Reading through Romans

Reading through Romans

C. R. Hume

SCM PRESS

0 334 02770 5

First published 1999 by
SCM Press
9–17 St Albans Place London N1 0NX

SCM Press is a division of
SCM-Canterbury Press Ltd

Typeset at The Spartan Press Ltd,
Lymington, Hants
Printed in Great Britain by
Biddles Ltd, Guildford and King's Lynn

Contents

Contents

Foreword

This is the fourth in a series of books on the letters of the New Testament in which I have aimed to provide straightforward guides explaining the original meaning of the text. I avoid, as far as is possible, entering into theological controversy. My priority is to establish the meaning, as I believe that we must study carefully the original text before we use it to support any doctrinal or theological viewpoint. Furthermore, as I state in the foreword to my first book in this series, *Reading through Hebrews*, I am concerned above all with what the text meant to a first-century reader. This is particularly necessary when studying the letter to the Romans, a document which has so often been interpreted in the light of contemporary concerns or obsessions.

Comments are based on my own translation of the text, because basing them on some one else's translation will only cause confusion, and because I can only defend my own translation; I cannot vouch for any one else's. I frequently focus on the meaning of particular Greek words, but these appear in a form which is easier for the non-Greek scholar to read.

Introduction

Why another book on Romans? In the first place, because most people, quite simply, believe it is the most important letter in the Pauline corpus, and one which contains some of the most moving passages in the New Testament. It has the unfortunate reputation of being the 'heaviest' of all Paul's letters, as one commentator puts it. That is as may be, but this reputation for difficulty could be partly accounted for by the fact that so many strong and famous personalities have written about this letter that we are in danger of seeing it only through their eyes. Over the years many commentators have attempted to read into the text and to discuss issues which may not actually be contained in the letter. I would justify writing yet another book on the grounds that it is time to reclaim Romans from those who have distorted its message, and I believe that we need to re-assess St Paul's teaching in the light of recent research and the historically more accurate interpretations which have appeared in the last few years. It may be hard to clear our minds of preconceptions and of the detritus of old battles, and to read this letter as though we have never seen it before, but it is worth the effort. I will need to touch upon some of the traditional problems associated with the interpretation of Romans, but I will try to be brief.

The origins of the church in Rome

There is plenty of evidence for the existence of a large community of Jews in Rome. Indeed, we know that they were expelled from the capital as early as 139 BC on the grounds that they were causing problems by their religious beliefs and practices. This expulsion had no long-term effect because a large number of them are known to be living there at the time of Julius Caesar. There were so many that, when they were expelled again during the reign of the emperor Tiberius, as many as four thousand of them, presumably younger men, were sent to fight bandits in Sardinia. The Jewish community re-established itself soon afterwards and we have archaeological evidence of the existence of many synagogues during the first century. Unlike Alexandria, where there was a large Jewish community under a central authority, the Roman Jews seem to have been more loosely organized.

The appearance of Christians in Rome during the reign of Claudius (41–54) is proved by the much-quoted statement of Suetonius that Claudius expelled the Jews because they were 'continually rioting due to the trouble-maker Chrestus', *assidue tumultuantes impulsore Chresto,*[1] an event dated to 49. As Wiefel argues,[2] this is a reference to Christ, albeit a garbled one. We know also from Acts 18.2 that Priscilla and Aquila were expelled from Rome about that time. When Paul meets them in Corinth, he treats them as people who were already Christians; they are not referred to as his converts. There is a tradition that Christianity had already been established amongst the Jews living in Rome before any official mission from the apostles. Ambrosiaster[3] says, 'So it is known that Jews lived in Rome in apostolic times, because

---

[1] *The Lives of the Twelve Caesars, Claudius* 25.
[2] *The Romans Debate*, ed. K. P. Donfried, T. & T. Clark 1991, 92.
[3] *Prologue to Commentary on Romans.*

they were under Roman rule. Those of them who had believed passed on to the Romans the tradition that they should keep the Law while professing Christ . . . One should not be angry with the Romans but rather praise their faith, because, without seeing any evidence of miracles, or any one of the apostles, they had accepted the faith of Christ, albeit with Jewish rites (*ritu licet Iudaico*).' On the death of Claudius, Jews (and presumably Jewish Christians) returned to Rome. We can deduce from the reference to Priscilla and Aquila in Rom. 16.3 that they were living in Rome again when Paul wrote his letter. There can be no doubt that they were joined by a large number of returning Jewish Christians who had not been converted by Paul, and who had not even met him. We can also assume that there were several Gentile Christians, some who had been originally converts to Judaism, and some who had gone straight from paganism to Christianity. Beker[4] argues not only that the church in Rome was mixed, but that the Gentiles were in the majority. This is not inconsistent with his statement that the main body of the letter confronts Judaism. I would prefer to substitute 'Judaizers' for 'Judaism', but we can let that pass. I also question the assumption that the Gentiles were in the majority, and will return to this subject later.

Authorship and date

There can be little reason for doubting the general consensus that Paul wrote this letter. Some commentators, however, have questioned the present form of the letter, whether it was originally written as one work or is a compilation, particularly in relation to the last chapter. For example, this chapter contains a long list of names, and some scholars have expressed doubts that Paul could have known so many people

---

[4] *Paul the Apostle*, T. & T. Clark, 1980, 75–6.

in a church which he had never visited. They have suggested that the final chapter belongs to an entirely different letter, perhaps one written originally to the church in Ephesus. It should be pointed out, however, that Paul sometimes adds no personal messages when he is writing to churches which he knows well, such as those in Galatia and Thessalonica. A much stronger argument for doubting the final chapter comes from the fact that some manuscripts put the doxology of 16.25–27 at the end of chapter 14. Some have it in both places, and one early papyrus even has it at the end of chapter 15. Two manuscripts omit it altogether. Even so, we should not jump to the conclusion that chapter 16 should be rejected. It is more likely that the variation in manuscripts is due to the fact that there were as many as three versions of the letter circulating in the early church: the original one, which is the one we use today; another shorter version which omitted the long list of personal names, probably because it was regarded as irrelevant; and one which omitted both chapters 15 and 16. There is certainly no evidence for the notion that Romans was designed originally by Paul as a circular letter to be sent to several churches, although it clearly was circulated, and, as Donfried points out,[5] there is now general agreement that Romans was addressed to the Christian community in Rome. Hence, he believes, chapter 16 is an integral part of that letter. We shall return to this point when we deal with that chapter.

The dating of the letter presents few problems, and most assume that it was written around the time when Paul wrote Galatians and II Corinthians, around 58. As I mentioned in my introduction to *Reading through Galatians*, Jerome saw the similarity of subject-matter in the letters to the Romans and the Galatians, but pointed out the difference in tone. The close links between the two letters have also led to the general

---

[5] *The Romans Debate*, ed. K. P. Donfried, T. & T. Clark 1991, 44–52.

acceptance by commentators that they were written about the same time.

Paul's reasons for writing this letter

As Wedderburn points out,[6] 'It has come to be widely recognized that Paul's letters are in large measure to be understood in the light of the context in which they were written.' It would be helpful if we knew to what sort of people Paul was writing. Let us start from the fact that they are a group of people whom he has never visited but many of whose names he seems to know. The long list of names which we find in chapter 16 might be an indication merely of the large number of Christian communities in Rome, or, more interestingly, of an intention on Paul's part to show that he was already familiar with an audience who might have resented someone who did not know them interfering in their affairs. As I have remarked above, it is a long list, longer than any list of names in any other letter. Some of these names, admittedly, belong to people whom Paul has met elsewhere, but it is clear that one powerful motive in writing this letter is to establish a closer relationship with all of the Christian groups in Rome. He carefully avoids giving the impression that he thinks they have faults which only he can remedy, or that he is asserting his control over them, yet he makes clear that he is imparting to them important information about their faith.

One of the reasons why Romans covers so much ground must be that Paul was anxious to leave them in no doubt about what the whole gospel message contained. After all, the Christian church in Rome had not been established and nurtured by Paul. Who could say what they had been taught or what gaps there might be in their knowledge of the gospel? It is not simply a friendly letter written for social reasons or

---

[6] *The Reasons for Romans*, T. & T. Clark 1988, 3.

one which was meant to soften them up for an appeal for funds to help the church in Jerusalem. If we look closely at the contents of the letter we can decipher Paul's concerns about the church in Rome. There were things happening there which certainly needed his advice, if not his criticism.

It is also possible to detect some of the criticisms which some Christians in Rome were voicing against Paul himself. For example, in chapter 1, as a preliminary to the main topics of his letter, we have a long list of the sins which incur God's judgment, and a clear condemnation of those sins. It is as though Paul is deliberately dissociating himself from a libertarian stance towards sin by emphasizing his disapproval. Throughout his life as an evangelist, Paul had to face the accusation from the Judaizers that he was an antinomian, against the Law, **nomos** (and by extension any moral law), and hence that he was tolerant towards sin. Paul refers to this charge in 3.8. Following this line of interpretation, Wedderburn suggests[7] that the main purpose of chapters 1–11 is 'to answer those criticisms of Paul's gospel and ministry which would prevent the Christians in Rome who had espoused a Judaizing form of Christianity from offering their support, their endorsement and their prayers for the success of his visit to Jerusalem with the collection'.

We can see also from Paul's references in chapter 15 to preaching the gospel in Spain another important reason to establish strong links with the Roman church. Rome would be a very convenient, if not necessary, base if he were to extend his operations to the western part of the Mediterranean.

The structure and message of the letter

Many commentators have felt obliged to look for a point in the letter which marks 'a sustained climax', as Robinson

---

[7] Ibid., 139.

describes it[8], locating it in chapter 8. Stendahl[9] speaks of chapters 9–11 as the climax, although it is hard to see how something as long as three chapters can constitute a climax. I believe that the search for a climax is based on the mistaken assumption that we are dealing with a work constructed according to classical literary criteria. If this were a tragedy of Aeschylus, say, we could look, as Aristotle recommends, for the **peripeteia**, i.e. the turning point on which the whole action of the drama hinges, but we are dealing with a letter, not a tragedy. Well then, can we at least say that there is a single theme? Beker[10] believes that it is a fallacy to claim that this letter has a single thematic unity. There is, admittedly, no reason why we should always look for either a climax or a single theme in a letter. Some letters are written to deal with one subject, but many are not. The search for a central core in Romans, according to Donfried[11] and Beker,[12] has led many commentators to focus on chapters 1–8 as the most important section of the letter, and to dismiss chapters 9–11 as an appendix or afterthought. But if the identification of a central core depends on the rejection of any part of the letter, we should be suspicious about the identification. We need not, however, rule out the possibility that there is a thread running through the letter which holds it together, and we can reasonably ask what are the main points which the writer is attempting to communicate.

It might help us in our search for these main points to ask to what extent this letter is similar to that addressed to the Galatians. In the first place, both letters are concerned with establishing that the Gentiles have an equal share in the

---

[8] *Wrestling with Romans*, SCM Press 1979, 9.

[9] *Paul among Jews and Gentiles*, SCM Press 1977, 4.

[10] *Paul the Apostle*, T. & T. Clark 1980, 71.

[11] *The Romans Debate*, ed. K. P. Donfried, T. & T. Clark 1991, Introduction.

[12] *Paul the Apostle*, T. & T. Clark 1980, 63–4.

promises given to Abraham. In the case of Galatians, Paul assures his mainly Gentile audience that they do not need to be circumcised and observe the *Torah*; i.e. they are not to think that, as Gentiles, they are at a disadvantage compared with the Jews, while in the case of the Romans, a mainly Jewish group, or at least one containing a large number of Jews, they are not to think that, as Jews, they have an advantage over the Gentiles. In other words, it is the same message, but one tailored to a different audience and a different situation. We might add that this same message underpins the anonymous letter to the Hebrews, another letter written for a Jewish audience, who, if I am correct in the argument I put forward in *Reading through Hebrews* (pp. 4–6), were also Jews living in Rome. Furthermore, the copious use of texts from the scriptures and the rabbinical method of using them, a phenomenon which also characterizes the letter to the Hebrews, points to the conclusion that the recipients of the letter to the Romans must have been largely Jewish, if not ethnically, at least culturally. In other words, they must have known the scriptures. So many commentators, in their obsession with *individual* justification, fail to recognize that the relation between Gentiles and Jews is central to all Paul's teaching. Hence there has been a tendency to underestimate the importance of, firstly, chapter 4 which deals with the subject of faithful Abraham as the one to whom the promises of God were made, and through whom all Christians, Jew or Gentile, are heirs of those promises, and, secondly, chapters 9–11 which explore the theme of Israel's place in God's scheme of salvation.

I have attempted in the following plan to show the structure of the letter.

1. *Introduction*

(1.1–7) Paul sends his greetings to the Christians in Rome and introduces himself.

(1.8–17) He thanks God for their faith and assures them that he prays continually for them and looks forward to visiting them and to preaching the gospel in Rome. This gospel of faith is for Jew and Gentile alike.

2. *The judgment of God*
(1.18–32) Human beings have turned away from God to commit all kinds of sins and will incur his judgment.
(2.1–16) Nobody, Jew or Greek, will escape the judgment of God, who will punish sins and reward good deeds. Those who have broken the Law will be judged by the Law. Gentile sinners outside the Law will also be punished.

3. *The position of Jews*
(2.17–29) Do not think that claiming to observe the Law will protect you. If you break the Law, you put yourself outside the Law.
(3.1–9) Jews were privileged to be entrusted with the word of God. The fact that some Jews are unfaithful does not cancel the faithful promises of God. The fact that human wickedness gives scope for the righteousness of God to operate does not mean that God should not punish it. Nor should we do evil so that good will come of it (that is what I am falsely accused of saying). Jews and Gentiles are equally sinful.
(3.10–18) Texts that witness to the fact that all have sinned.
(3.19–31) No one is justified by the works of the Law, but only by faith in Jesus Christ who has expiated our sins. God is God of both the Gentiles and the Jews.

4. *The importance of Abraham*
(4.1–25) How Abraham's faith in God provides the pattern for the justification of all mankind through faith.

5. *The results of justification*
(5. 1–5) The effects on us who believe.

(5. 6–11) Jesus died for us while we were sinners and saved us from the wrath.

(5.12–21) As death came into the world through one man's sin, so life is restored by one man's righteousness.

6. *Our relationship to sin*

(6.1–14) It is a mistake to assume that continuing to sin increases grace. When we were baptized we died to sin and were set free from sin. Having died with Christ we hope to share his life. Do not let sin have any power over you. You are under the rule of grace, not the Law.

(6.15–23) Being under grace and not the Law does not mean we can sin. To serve sin leads to death; to serve obedience leads to righteousness. Being freed from sin, you were made the servants of righteousness. As you once served sin and were unclean, so you must serve righteousness and be holy. Sin results in death, but God has given us eternal life through Christ.

7. *The rule of the Law*

(7.1–4) The effect of death on the obligations of the marriage contract as an illustration of our obligations in regard to the Law.

(7.5–14) The relationship between sin and the Law.

(7.15–25) The psychological effects of sin and the conflict between the Law and sin.

8. *The liberation from sin through Christ and the gift of the Holy Spirit*

(8. 1–13) Christ has freed us from the Law and from sin and death. The victory of the Spirit over the flesh gives life.

(8.14–17) We are the children of God and heirs with Christ of future glory.

(8.18–39) We shall be delivered from our sufferings. We look forward patiently in hope. The Spirit assists us in ways we

cannot comprehend. God has determined to save us. Nothing
can stand in his way.

9. *The place of Israel in God's scheme of salvation*
(9.1–21) Paul longs for the salvation of the people who were
given a special role by God, although it is God's choice who
will be saved. He has the right to decide on whom he will have
mercy. The creature cannot question the creator's reasons for
making him what he is.

(9.22–33) God has put up with the disobedience of his people
long enough and has decided to show mercy to people who
were not originally his people. Nevertheless, he will save a
remnant of Israel. Only those who are justified by faith, not by
the works of the Law, shall be saved, whether they be Jew or
Gentile.

(10.1–13) Paul wishes that his people would be saved, but
Christ is the only way by which this can happen. All they need
to do is believe that Christ was raised from the dead and
confess him as Lord. There is no difference between Jew and
Gentile. All who call upon the Lord will be saved.

(10.14–21) They cannot believe in Christ if they have not
heard about him. But they *have* heard. They were also warned
by the prophets that if they were disobedient, God would
choose another people.

(11.1–10) God has not cast off his people entirely, but
preserved a faithful remnant, as an act of grace, not as a
reward for performing some service. The rest have been
hardened and are not members of his elect.

(11.11–15) Nevertheless, there is a hope that they too will be
saved, by their jealousy of the Gentiles. Their transgression
has brought the Gentiles salvation. How wonderful it will be
when all of Israel accepts the gospel!

(11.16–24) The metaphors of the first offering and the olive
tree: the Gentiles should not forget that they owe their new
status to the holy patriarchs and prophets, and that they share

this privileged position with their fellow Jewish Christians. They should take nothing for granted. They can just as easily lose it. Similarly, the Jews who have not yet accepted Christ can return to their natural place.

(11.25–36) God intends to rescue all his people when the Gentiles have been fully perfected. They may be hostile to the gospel now, but they are still loved because of their fore-fathers. God is merciful to everyone, even though everyone has been unfaithful. How inscrutable are God's ways!

10. *An exhortation to holiness*

(12.1–21) Present yourselves to God as a holy sacrifice. Follow the will of God. Do not think too much of yourselves. Let us all exercise our different gifts in the church. Love one another, do not be idle, be hopeful and patient, pray, be generous, do not return evil for evil, be sympathetic, live in peace. Do not be vindictive.

(13.1–14) Respect authority and obey the law. Keep the commandments, especially the main one – love your neigh-bour as yourself. The day of the Lord is at hand. Be vigilant.

11. *Problems of conscience and conforming*

(14.1–7) Accept the scruples of others regarding food or rites based on a religious calendar and, if you have scruples yourselves, do not impose them on others. Do whatever you do for the Lord's sake.

(14.8–13) Whether we are alive or dead we belong to Christ, Lord of the living and the dead. We shall all stand at his judgment seat and give an account of ourselves. So do not judge your fellow Christians, but rather avoid putting ob-stacles in their way.

(14.14–23) Nothing is unclean in itself, but if you feel it is unclean, it is unclean to you. If someone is offended at your liberal attitude towards food laws, you are not behaving with love. The kingdom of God, which is righteousness, peace and joy in the Spirit, is more important than food and drink. Go for peace and do not let your diet destroy God's work. Although all things are clean, it is best to avoid eating or drinking anything which causes problems for your fellow Christian. Do not eat or drink anything if it troubles your conscience to do so.

(15.1–13) We who are not troubled by scruples should consider our weaker brethren. Christ did not please himself – nor should you. Take hope from the scriptures. Christ was sent to unite Jews and Gentiles, to fulfil the scriptures for the former and to bring the latter into God's mercy. May God fill you with joy, peace and hope!

12. *Paul's special mission and his plans for the future*

(15. 14–17) I know that you are quite capable of understanding the faith, but I have written to you because God has given me the grace to preach his gospel. My special mission is to the Gentiles.

(15.18–33) So far I have preached from Jerusalem to Illyricum, and only in places where Christ's gospel has not already been proclaimed. I have always wanted to visit you and hope to see you when I go to Spain. Meanwhile I have to go to Jerusalem with funds for the poor there. Please pray that I may perform my task successfully and safely and finally be able to visit you.

13. *Final words and personal greetings*

(16.1–23) Paul commends the bearer of his letter, Phoebe, and lists those to whom he wishes to send his regards, and those who send their regards.

(16.24–27) Final prayer.

A few things to note

1. Certain abbreviations are used throughout this book.

AV	Authorized Version
NEB	New English Bible
NT	New Testament
OT	Old Testament
Sept.	Septuagint
Vulg.	Vulgate (the Latin version of the Bible by St Jerome).

2. Besides modern writers, whose works are listed at the end of the guide, I have consulted various ancient scholars, most of whom are listed in the biographies below.

Biographies

Ambrosiaster. So called because his commentaries on Paul's letters were wrongly ascribed to St Ambrose. It is generally believed that he is Hilary the Roman deacon who lived around the middle of the fourth century and wrote sometime during the pontificate of Damasus (366–384).

Augustine (354–430). Bishop of Hippo in north Africa, who was converted to Christianity from Manichaeism and whose most famous works are his *Confessions* and *The City of God*.

Jerome (around 345–420). Studied in Rome and spent some time in Constantinople with Gregory of Nazianzus. Settled in Bethlehem where he founded four monastic communities. Attacked Pelagianism. Famous for his translation of the Bible into Latin. Wrote a commentary on Romans.

John Chrysostom 'Golden-mouth' (around 349–407), famous

for his preaching. Delivered his homilies on Romans in Antioch before he became bishop of Constantinople. Died in exile after offending the empress Eudoxia.

Clement of Rome (died around 100). Third or fourth bishop of Rome and reputedly a disciple of Paul and Peter. Wrote at least one letter to the Corinthians. The second letter to the Corinthians attributed to him is most probably by a later writer.

Justin Martyr (around 100–165). Born in Samaria. As a young man he studied Platonist and Stoic philosophers. After his conversion he wrote two *Apologies for the Christians* and the *Dialogue with Trypho the Jew*. Martyred during the reign of the emperor Marcus Aurelius.

Lucian (around 117–180). From Samosata in Syria. Started as a lawyer but took up literature and gave public recitations. His work, which is largely satire or comedy, covers contemporary life and frequently takes the form of dramatic dialogue. His references to Christianity gave him the reputation of being an enemy of the faith, although he says little which would cause offence today.

Marcion (around 100–160). From Sinope in the province of Pontus. Denounced as a heretic, he founded his own sect. In essence, he divided God into two, an evil God of the Law and a good God revealed in Jesus Christ. Hence he rejected the Jewish scriptures and only accepted those parts of the New Testament which fitted in with his doctrines.

Origen (around 185–254). Christian Platonist and biblical scholar. His works were used extensively by Jerome when writing his commentaries. We have only a few fragments of the original Greek; the main part survives in a Latin translation. Taught first in Alexandria and then Palestine, where he was ordained priest. Imprisoned and tortured during the Decian persecutions.

Pliny (the Younger) (around 61–113). Governor of Bithynia, where he had occasion to consult the emperor Trajan about his policy towards Christianity. Famous for his letters and his eye-witness account of the eruption of Vesuvius.

Philo (around 30 BC–AD 45). Head of Jewish community in Alexandria. Sent as delegate to Rome to ask the emperor Caligula for exemption from duty of worshipping emperor. Combined Judaism with Greek philosophy, particularly Platonism. Prolific writer on subjects connected with scripture and theology.

Suetonius (around AD 69–140). Roman citizen of equestrian rank. After practising briefly at the bar he became secretary to the emperor Hadrian. After being dismissed by the emperor he spent his time writing. The only work of his to survive is the *Lives of the Twelve Caesars*, a work containing much valuable material which he obtained from his access to imperial archives.

Tertullian (around 160–225). Trained as a lawyer. Spent most of his life in Carthage. Most important for his ability to express Christian terms in Latin. Defended Christianity against pagans and Jews and expounded Christian doctrine and practice in the church. Later joined the strict Montanist sect.

Chapter 1

1 Paul, a slave of Christ Jesus, called as an apostle, set apart for the gospel of God, 2 which he proclaimed beforehand through his prophets in the holy scriptures 3 concerning his son who was born of the seed of David according to the flesh, 4 and who was ordained the son of God with power according to the Spirit of holiness following his resurrection from the dead, Jesus Christ our Lord,

[1] The first thing Paul does is to establish his own credentials: he is 'called', **klêtos**, and 'set apart', **aphôrismenos**, by God, as Jerome says, 'to preach to the Gentiles'. These terms recall Gal. 1.15, 'God, *who ordained* (**aphorisâs**) me from my mother's womb, and *called* (**kalesâs**) me through his grace . . .' 'Set apart' denotes consecration for a special purpose, as Acts 13.2 makes clear, '*set apart* (**aphorisate**) for me Barnabas and Saul for the work to which *I have called* (**proskeklêmai**) them'. It does not mean here that he was socially segregated or set on a pedestal, as the Vulg. *segregatus* might suggest.

'The gospel of God' is defined by Jerome as the account of Christ's 'nativity, his passion, his resurrection and his ascension to heaven'.

[2, 3] Secondly, Paul relates his message, the gospel of Christ,

to the OT prophecies regarding the Messiah. This was the
standard approach used by the apostles when preaching to a
Jewish audience and the one used by Peter when he first
proclaimed the gospel in Jerusalem on the day of Pentecost
(Acts 2.14–36). Paul clearly is writing to an audience which
we might assume to be Gentiles from the way in which he
refers to them in v. 6, but must have been a mixture of Jews
and Gentile proselytes who knew the scriptures. The Cor-
inthian church, in contrast, seems to be largely from a pagan
background. It is interesting that Peter also referred to the
descent of Jesus from David, a fact emphasized by the
genealogies of Matthew and Luke and mentioned in John
7.42 and Rev. 22.16.

'According to the flesh', i.e. 'in a physical sense', 'on the
human level'.

[4] 'Ordained', **horisthentos**, from the verb **horizô**, from
which we derive the word 'horizon', i.e. 'that which defines
a boundary'. This verb is common in Acts in the sense of
'mark out' or 'ordain', but rare elsewhere in the NT. Outside
Acts it occurs only here, in Luke (22.22), and in Hebrews
(4.7). This verse should not be interpreted as implying that
Jesus only became the son of God, or that he only received the
Holy Spirit, 'the Spirit of holiness', after he was resurrected;
he was already God's son. The emphasis is on the phrase
'with power'. After God raised Christ in glory the Holy Spirit
could be poured out on his followers, so that they were
enabled to share Christ's power. As a result, Christ was
openly 'marked out' as God's son. Chrysostom explains
'ordained' as 'shown, manifested, judged, confessed by the
opinion and vote of everyone, from the prophets, from his
miraculous birth in the flesh, from the power in his miracles,
from the Spirit, through whom he gave sanctification, from
the resurrection, through which he destroyed the tyranny of
death'. Lightfoot suggests that the resurrection referred to is

not Christ's but the general resurrection of the dead, 'which was implied in His Resurrection and of which His Resurrection was the firstfruits and the assurance', but this can hardly be the meaning here.

5 through whom we have received grace and apostleship for the hearing of the faith among all the nations for his name's sake, 6 among whom you, too, are called to belong to Jesus Christ, 7 to all who are in Rome beloved of God, called [as] saints, grace to you and peace from God our Father and the Lord Jesus Christ.

[5] 'For the hearing of the faith', **eis hypakoên pisteôs**, a phrase repeated in 16.26, is reminiscent of the phrase **ex akoês pisteôs**, 'from a response to faith', found in Gal. 3.2. See my notes on this verse in *Reading through Galatians*. **Hypakoê**, which the AV renders as 'obedience', seems here to be almost a synonym for **akoê**, 'hearing'. It refers, however, not just to the hearing of the faith, but to the response of believers to the gospel which they have heard. Barclay translates the phrase as 'to awaken a faithful obedience', but this does not make explicit enough the connection between Paul's apostleship and the preaching of the gospel. In other words, 'apostleship for the hearing of the faith' is an abbreviated way of saying 'to act as an apostle in spreading the good news so that people might hear and believe'.

'The nations', **tois ethnesin**, could also be translated as 'the Gentiles', but see the next note.

[6] 'Among whom', i.e. the nations, should not be taken as implying that his audience must have consisted entirely of Gentiles. Paul is probably thinking of the diverse nationalities of his audience who happen to have come together in Rome.

The Jews among his audience are obviously from different
parts of the Roman empire, just as the Gentiles are.

'Called to belong to Jesus Christ', rather than the AV's
literal 'called of Jesus Christ', which would mean to us 'called
by Jesus Christ'. Paul generally assumes that we are called by
God the Father.

[7] 'In Rome' is omitted by one late manuscript both here and
also in v. 15. This is further evidence for the suggestion
mentioned in the introduction, namely, that there were
versions of this letter circulating which did not contain local
references. Note that there is no mention of a church. This
would suggest that there were several communities of Christians in Rome, and that Paul is writing to a diverse group of
separate communities.

'Grace' and 'peace' are part of Paul's greetings in all his
letters. See my notes on Gal. 1.3 in *Reading through
Galatians*.

8 Firstly, I thank my God through Jesus Christ for all
of you, in that your faith is reported throughout the
whole world. 9 For God is my witness, he whom I
serve with my spirit in the gospel of his son, that I do
not cease to mention you 10 at all times in my prayers,
asking that I may somehow sometime by God's will at
last manage to visit you. 11 For I long to see you in
order that I may share with you some spiritual
blessing which will strengthen you, 12 that is, that
will give me as well as you mutual encouragement
through the faith that you and I have in common.

[8] Paul regularly expresses his gratitude to God for the
spiritual progress of the recipients of his letters. It is hardly
surprising that he expresses no such sentiments when he

writes to the Galatians. Jerome makes the point that there are two ways of taking this verse: either the faith displayed by the Romans is famous everywhere, or the same faith which the Romans profess is being preached everywhere. In other words, Paul is not necessarily praising the Romans.

[9] 'With my spirit', **en tôi pneumati mou**, could mean either 'with my whole heart' or 'in the spiritual gift which I have been given'. Barrett suggests, 'it is by using his spirit, in the field of activities proper to the spiritual side of his nature, that Paul renders God service'.

[10] 'Manage', **euodôthêsomai**, literally, 'have a good journey', 'fare well', hence 'succeed'.

[11] 'Blessing', **charisma**, from 'grace', **charis**. **Charisma** is the word used in chapter 12 of I Corinthians to describe the spiritual 'gifts' or 'favours' freely bestowed on individual Christians by God. The word is as rich in meaning as the commoner word **charis**, on which see my notes on Gal. 1.3 in *Reading through Galatians* and on Heb. 12.28 in *Reading through Hebrews*.

'Which will strengthen you', literally, 'for you to be made firm', **eis to stêrichthênai hûmâs**. The verb **stêrizô** means 'fix, make fast', hence 'establish'. In medical writers it is used to describe the action of 'building up' a patient.

[12] 'That will give me as well as you mutual encouragement', literally, '[for me] to be encouraged together in you'. Jerome paraphrases this verse, 'that we may encourage one another by our shared faith', *ut per communem fidem invicem consolemur.*

13 I do not want you, brothers and sisters, to be

ignorant [of the fact] that I often intended to visit you,
but was prevented so far [from doing so], so that I
might gain some profitable return also among you just
as among the other nations. 14 I am a debtor to
Greeks and barbarians, to wise and foolish people; 15
hence my eagerness to preach the gospel to you in
Rome too. 16 For I am not ashamed of the gospel; it is
the power of God for salvation to every believer, to
the Jew first, and [then] also the Greek. 17 For the
righteousness of God is revealed in it from faith to
faith; as it has been written, 'the just through faith
shall live'.

[13] 'Gain some profitable return', literally, 'have some fruit'.
This could be 'have some enjoyment', but it is more likely to
mean 'produce some good results'.

'Nations' rather than the AV 'Gentiles' here for the reasons
outlined in the note on v. 6. 'Gentiles' would imply that Paul
was only writing to non-Jews, whereas several chapters
clearly contain material specifically addressed to Jews.

[14] 'I am a debtor', as Barclay points out, has two meanings:
the writer is saying, firstly, that he owes a great deal because
of the kindnesses he has received and, secondly, that he is
under an obligation to preach the gospel to everyone.

'Greeks and barbarians' and 'wise and foolish' are difficult
phrases. Does the first phrase mean 'Greek speakers and non-
Greek speakers', which is the usual meaning in Greek
literature? Jerome takes 'Greeks' as a synonym for 'wise',
and 'barbarians' as meaning the same as 'foolish'. Barclay
seems to take the two phrases as meaning 'cultured and
uncultured, lettered and unlettered', while Dodd takes the
latter as 'educated and uneducated'. I would suggest 'Greek

speakers and non-Greek speakers, educated and simple people alike'. The problem is made more complicated by the fact that the Romans are technically barbarians because their normal language is Latin, yet Paul is writing to this group in Rome in Greek. Greek continued to be the main language of the church even in the West for many years, and this fact causes one to ask whether the early church particularly attracted members with an eastern Mediterranean background. Certainly Rome was a bilingual city with a large number of slaves and craftsmen living there who had come from Greek-speaking areas of the empire, and with an educated class who frequently used Greek in private conversations and in letters. We cannot conclude from the Latin names of Christians mentioned in the New Testament that they were from a Latin-speaking background any more than we can assume that an English name means that its owner is of Anglo-Saxon descent. Latin names conferred respectability and aligned the owner with the political ascendancy. Indeed, slaves who were given their freedom received the Latin names of their owners. So, in using the phrase 'Greeks and barbarians', Paul is unlikely to be assigning his audience to one of the two categories. It is more likely that he is using the term loosely to make a general point, namely, that he is obliged to preach the gospel throughout the whole world and to every nation.

[15] 'Hence my eagerness', literally 'thus the eager[ness] as far as I am concerned', **houtôs to kat'eme prothûmon**. In other words, Paul is saying that if it were up to him he would be in Rome now. It is external factors which have prevented him from visiting them, not reluctance on his part.

[16] 'The power of God for salvation' can be paraphrased as 'the means by which God can save'.

'To the Jew first, and [then] also the Greek', a phrase which occurs also in 2.9 and 2.10, echoes the sentiment expressed in

Eph. 1.12, where the writer refers to himself and other Jewish Christians as 'the ones who were first to place our hope in Christ'. Paul alludes again to this in 15.8, 9, 'For I say that Christ has been made a minister of the circumcision for God's truth, in order to confirm the promises of [our] fathers, and so that the Gentiles may glorify God for his mercy.' Note that 'Greek' here is opposed to 'Jew', not 'barbarian', and so is a synonym for 'Gentile', someone from a pagan background.

[17] This verse plunges us into one of the major subjects of this letter. Is the 'righteousness of God', **dikaiosynê Theou**, God's own righteousness or the righteousness he bestows, the justice that he executes or the justification he confers on sinners? We cannot answer such a question without first examining the word **dikaiosynê**. Commentators have tended to talk about the word 'justification', **dikaiôsis**, but **dikaiôsis** only occurs twice in the whole of the NT, in Rom. 4.25 and 5.18. **Dikaiosynê**, on the other hand, occurs 92 times, 33 times in Romans alone. It is the abstract noun of the adjective **dikaios**, 'just' or 'righteous', which gives us also the verb **dikaioô**, 'I justify'. For the meanings of these last two words see my notes on Gal. 2.16 in *Reading through Galatians*. **Dikaiosynê** is not only the characteristic attribute of God, it is also the principal activity of God which is recorded in scripture. The account of God in the OT is largely a description of the way in which he displays his righteousness; see my note on Heb. 5.13 in *Reading through Hebrews*. In the OT God is frequently portrayed as vindicating or delivering his people. This activity is God's righteousness. For example, Judges 5.11 (AV), 'They that are delivered from the noise of archers in the places of drawing water, there shall they rehearse the *righteous acts* (Sept. **dikaiosynâs**) of the Lord.' In other words, God restores and upholds the right or just state of affairs and he dispenses justice. He is also faithful and keeps his promises. It is not surprising, therefore, to find that

salvation and righteousness are frequently associated. For instance, Isa. 51.5 (Sept.), 'My righteousness draws swiftly near, and my salvation shall go forth as a light.' As Wright points out (*What Saint Paul Really Said*, 97), 'righteousness' is a forensic term, and when applied to the judge means that he is impartial and upholds the law. He punishes the guilty and vindicates the innocent and defenceless. For the defendant to be 'righteous', **dikaios**, he has to be acquitted of the charge, to be declared 'not guilty'. Those who are 'justified' in this way are placed in a right relationship with God; they are 'just', **dikaioi**. Hence we can frequently translate **dikaiosynê** as 'justification'.

'In it' refers to the gospel. Paul is speaking of the doctrine of justification by faith which is at the heart of the gospel.

'From faith to faith' has been described as a rhetorical figure emphasizing the word 'faith', but it is clearly more than that. Before we discuss the meaning of the phrase we should remind ourselves that 'faith', **pistis**, as I point out in my notes on Gal. 3.9 in *Reading through Galatians* and on Heb. 11.6 in *Reading through Hebrews*, carries a very wide range of meanings, including the active sense of faith which trusts in someone else and the passive sense denoting faithfulness in which trust is placed. The following interpretations have been suggested:

1. 'from the faith (of the believer responding) to the faithfulness (of God)'.
2. '(which comes) *through* faith (in Jesus Christ) and *to* (all who have such) faith'. This is suggested by Robinson, commenting on 3.21–26 but referring back to this verse.
3. 'on the basis of nothing but faith'. This is Barrett's translation of the phrase, but in his notes he explains this as 'faith from start to finish', which seems much more like the next interpretation. Similarly Käsemann says, 'The revelation of God's righteousness, because it is

bound to the gospel, takes place always only in the sphere of faith.'

4. 'from faith *leading on* to faith'. In other words, from the first act of believing one is led on a continual journey of faith; as the NEB puts it, 'a way that starts from faith and ends in faith'. Lightfoot also explains the phrase in a similar way, 'Faith is the starting point, and faith the goal.' Sanday and Headlam put forward a variation of this interpretation and claim that the phrase means 'starting from a smaller quantity of faith to produce a larger quantity'. As believers progress on their journey, they see and understand more and more the righteousness of God.

I am not convinced by any of these interpretations, although the fourth is the best, and prefer to take the phrase 'from faith to faith' as referring to the different examples of faith described in scripture, i.e. 'one example of faith after another', which culminate in faith in Christ which is revealed 'in it', i.e. 'in the gospel'. Chrysostom, as so often happens, supplies the missing clue: 'By saying "from faith to faith" he has sent the hearer back to the dispensations of God, which occurred in the Old Testament, and which, in his letter to the Hebrews, he explains with great wisdom, showing that both righteous and sinners were justified in this way (i.e. by faith) even then.' This may also be the meaning lurking behind Jerome's cryptic comment, *quod ex fide iustificatur Iudaeus, et in fide Gentilis*, 'because the Jew is justified from faith, and the Gentile in faith'. We can see what Chrysostom means when we look at chapter 11 of Hebrews, where verse after verse starts with 'by faith', followed by the names of the various patriarchs and matriarchs, who showed their trust in God by specific acts of faith. So Paul seems to be saying that the salvation which is now revealed through faith in Christ was preceded by many examples of faith in which the righteousness of God was revealed in the scriptures. Abraham believed and was given the great promises, Sarah conceived a child, Noah was saved from the flood and Moses escaped from Egypt. As we read in Heb. 11.32–34, 'And what more shall I say? For the time would fail me to tell of Gideon, Barak, Samson, Jephthah, of David and Samuel and the prophets, who, through faith conquered kingdoms, dispensed justice, won promises, stopped the mouths of lions, quenched the power of fire, escaped the edge of the sword, were empowered out of weakness, became strong in war and turned aside the armies of the aliens.'

'The just through faith shall live', rather than the AV 'The just shall live by faith'. This key text from Habakkuk 2.4, quoted also in Gal. 3.11, is an abbreviation of the original Septuagint text, which has **mou**, 'of/in me' after 'faith'. Hebrews 10.38, incidentally, quotes the text with **mou**. Paul, as in Galatians, clearly takes the text as saying that the one who is justified by faith will receive life, not merely that the just man will live a life trusting in God.

18 For the anger of God is revealed from heaven against every impiety and wickedness of human beings who, in their wickedness, suppress the truth, 19 since that which is known of God is obvious among them; for God has revealed it to them. 20 For from the foundation of the world they have perceived through his deeds, when they reflect on them, his invisible [attributes], namely, his unseen power and divinity; so they have no excuse, 21 because, although they knew God, they neither glorified him as God nor thanked him, but made fools of themselves with their debates and their stupid hearts were darkened.

[18] The 'anger of God' is a recurrent theme in this letter, but it also occurs in other letters, for example, Eph. 5.6 and Col. 3.6. The NT nowhere says of God that he is angry, but the phrase 'anger of God' occurs nine times. In most cases it is virtually a synonym for the judgment of God which will be meted out on the last day. 'Anger' can also refer to secular judgment by civil authorities, as in 13.4 and 5. Note that the verb 'is revealed', which we have met in v. 17, is repeated here. Just as the previous verse refers to examples of God justifying and delivering the faithful, so this verse tells us that we can expect him to condemn and punish the unfaithful. The use of the present tense, 'is revealed', which means 'has been revealed in the past and is still being revealed' (see below the note on tense in v. 20), implies that Paul is talking not only about a future judgment but about the fact that his audience already knows what God's judgment will be: in other words, they cannot be ignorant of his disapproval of vice, since scripture, in particular, records many examples of God punishing wickedness when his people committed acts which brought down his anger. In vv. 24–28 Paul clearly refers to such punishment as taking place in a contemporary situation.

'Impiety', **asebeian**, literally, 'dishonouring' or 'irreverence'.

'Wickedness', **adikiân**, i.e. 'injustice', the opposite of **dikaiosynê**. Note the deliberate repetition of the noun in this verse.

'Suppress', **katechontôn**, a verb which has two diametrically opposed meanings, 'hold back', hence 'hamper' or 'withhold', as we have here, and 'hold fast', hence 'keep' or 'observe', as in Heb. 3.14 and 10.23. The truth which they suppress is most probably the knowledge of God referred to in the next two verses, but it could be a synonym for 'righteousness', i.e. 'true judgment', as it is in 2.8. In other words, they are acting unjustly.

[19] 'That which is known of God' is another way of saying 'as far as we can know anything about God' or 'that which God allows human beings to know about him', since God is beyond our comprehension.

'Among them', **en autois**, or alternatively, 'within them', i.e., as Sanday and Headlam suggest, 'in their thoughts', *in conscientiis eorum*, as Jerome says.

[20] Faith in the unseen God is a familiar idea in Jewish thought. As Heb. 11.6, 7 says, 'for the one who approaches God must have believed both that he exists, and that he rewards those who seek him out. By faith Noah was warned of things that had not yet been seen, and reverently constructed an ark to save his household.' This knowledge is twofold: firstly, God created and rules the world, and secondly, he upholds righteousness; that is, his 'unseen power' operates at the material and the moral level. His 'divinity' is unseen, because God cannot be seen and because it is apprehended by faith. We can also add that the Jew believed that if one were to see God one would die.

'They have perceived through his deeds, when they reflect on them, his invisible [attributes]', literally, 'his unseen [things] by his deeds being pondered on are seen'. The notion that the unseen God is seen through his deeds is also found in Greek pagan philosophy: for instance, Pseudo-Aristotle (*On the Cosmos*, 399b) states, 'although he is *invisible* (**atheôrêtos**) to every mortal nature *he is seen* (**theôreitai**) from his actual deeds'. The verb 'are seen', represented in my translation by 'they have perceived', is present tense but really means 'have been seen and are still being seen'. As I point out in *Reading through Colossians and Ephesians* in my notes on Col. 1.17, in English we often use a special tense to refer to an action which started in the past and is still going on. Hence, 'I have been waiting' means 'I started waiting some time ago and am still waiting'.

[21] 'Made fools of themselves', **emataiôthêsan**, a verb formed from the adjective **mataios**, which covers a wide range of meanings, such as 'idle', 'futile', 'worthless', 'irreverent', 'rash' and 'profane'.

'Debates', **dialogismois**, can also be translated as 'speculations' or 'calculations'.

'Hearts', or rather 'heart', because it occurs here in the singular, is often used where we would expect 'minds'. In the ancient world the heart was not thought of as merely the seat of the emotions. It also housed the faculty of thought and intellect.

22 While claiming to be wise, they became foolish 23 and altered the glory of the immortal God by likening him to the image of a mortal human being, and of winged, four-footed and creeping [animals]. 24 As a result, God delivered them up in the desires of their hearts to the filthiness of dishonouring their bodies among themselves, 25 [people] who exchanged the truth of God for falsehood, and who worshipped and revered the creature rather than the creator, who is blessed for ever, amen.

[22, 23] The link between idolatry and foolishness is obvious if we remember that for the Jew, or the monotheistic pagan philosopher, it was patently absurd to treat anything created, especially an image, as though it were comparable to the Creator. It is worth remembering, too, that 'foolishness' is not just a failing of the intellect; it is also a moral fault. By deliberately rejecting the truth and choosing a lie, one has committed a sin, not just an error of judgment.

'Creeping' covers such things as alligators and snakes as well as insects. There was no sharp distinction between the ostensible anthropomorphism of Roman and Greek pagans, who tended to claim the moral high ground, and such cultures as that of the Egyptians, who worshipped cows, alligators and ibises. Everywhere Paul went he would have seen altars and shrines depicting snakes as tutelary or ancestral spirits and encountered local cult centres where the Olympian deities were worshipped in animal form or even as meteorites. There is, therefore, no need to accept Lightfoot's contrast of the anthropomorphic mythologies of Greece and Rome with the animal worship of Assyria and Egypt or Käsemann's assertion that the last part of v. 23 refers specifically to the Egyptian religion. Jerome, for example, mentions the various metamorphoses into animal forms which Jupiter underwent in his sexual pursuits, *propter amores foedissimos*.

[24] 'As a result', **dio**, i.e. 'because of which', Vulg. *propter quod*; it may seem odd to us that idolatry should inevitably lead to sexual immorality, but pagan festivals and rituals frequently encouraged, and sometimes obliged, worshippers to perform acts which would not normally be condoned. Bowdlerized and sentimental teaching about the classical world has blurred our vision of paganism. Jerome, who knew at first hand what paganism was really like, says, quoting from Wisdom 14.27, 'for the worship of unspeakable idols is the cause, beginning and end of every evil'.

'Delivered up', **paredôken**, as Barclay points out, is not to be interpreted as an act of anger or irritation. It is allowing people to exercise their free will. In fact, as Eph. 4.19 says, *'they have abandoned themselves* (**heautous paredôkan**) to outrageous behaviour, to practise every kind of filthiness in excess'.

'Desires', **epithûmiais**, are often described as 'fleshly', 'of the flesh', as in Gal. 5.16 and Eph. 2.3, and associated with sexual sins, as in Col. 3.5 and I Thess. 4.5. **Epithûmiâ**, however, is in itself a morally neutral word, as we can seen in Luke 22.15, 'With desire have I desired (**epithûmiâi epethûmêsa**) to eat this passover with you before I suffer.'

'Filthiness', **akatharsiân**, is immoral sexual activity, or, as Jerome says, 'filthiness which occurs in the vile rituals of idols'. See my notes on Col. 3.5 in *Reading through Colossians and Ephesians*.

'Of dishonouring their bodies' is interpreted by both Chrysostom and Jerome as actual mutilations inflicted on those participating in pagan rites. Chrysostom says, 'they did not need others to do violence to them, since they did to themselves the very things which their enemies would have done to them'. Jerome speaks of *cauteria et combustiones*, which could refer to branding. Paul's audience would have been familiar with the spectacle of the priests of Cybele castrating themselves in their frenzy.

[25] 'Truth' could be taken here in the sense of 'reality', i.e. true nature, or as denoting 'righteousness'. See my notes on 2.8.

'Creature', or 'creation', **ktisei**.

'Who is blessed for ever, amen' is a short praise formula, a pious interjection.

26 For this reason, God delivered them up to disgraceful passions, for women exchanged their natural practice for an unnatural one, 27 and similarly, men, too, gave up their natural relationship with women and were consumed with their passion for one another, men practising obscenities with men and receiving in their own persons the reward due to them for their perversity. 28 And just as they rejected the knowledge of God, God delivered them up to their reprobate minds, to do things which are not right,

[26] 'Disgraceful passions', literally, 'passions of dishonour', **pathê atîmiâs**.

'Unnatural', i.e. lesbianism, because it corresponds to the homosexual practices of men referred to in the next verse.

[27] 'Relationship', **chrêsin**, literally, 'use'. In the previous verse I translate this word as 'practice'.

'Were consumed', **exekauthêsan**, literally, 'were burnt out'.

'Practising obscenities', **tên aschêmosynên katergazomenoi**, literally, 'achieving ugliness'.

What is this 'reward'? Because the main verb is in the past tense it is unlikely that it is the punishment awaiting them at the final judgment; it is a reward that they have already received. Chrysostom mentions the destruction of Sodom specifically as a punishment for homosexual activities. It could be that Paul is referring, as Chrysostom suggests, to those punished when Sodom was destroyed by fire, but he may be referring to his contemporaries. In this case, the phrase 'in their own persons', literally, 'in themselves', **en heautois**, could refer to the physical effects of their sexual activities, i.e. disease or injuries, or it could include social disadvantages and impaired life-style. Some states imposed legal penalties on practising homosexuals and it is possible that this is what Paul has in mind.

[28] There is a word play in Greek, which it is difficult to reproduce in English, between 'they rejected', **ouk edokimasan**, and 'reprobate', **adokimon**. The verb means 'test', hence 'approve'. So **ouk edokimasan** means 'they did not approve after scrutiny'. **Adokimon** means 'not approved', and was used to describe coinage that was not legal tender. Hence a person so described is 'disreputable', 'discredited'. Paul is making the point that by rejecting God they became rejects themselves.

'The knowledge of God', literally, 'to have God *in recognition* (**en epignôsei**)'. **Epignôsis** occurs three times in Romans and twice is used, as in Ephesians and Colossians (Col. 1.9,

1.10, 2.2; Eph. 1.17, 4.13), in reference to 'knowing' God or Christ. Although it seems to be a synonym for **gnôsis**, it is particularly appropriate when it refers to the knowledge of God because it also denotes 'getting to know' or 'recognizing' a person.

29 being full of every injustice, wickedness, excess and malice, laden with envy, murder, strife, deceit and spitefulness, whispering slander, 30 spreading evil stories, hating God, wantonly violent, arrogant, impostors, inventors of evil, with no obedience towards parents, 31 with no understanding, with no intention of keeping their word, with no natural affection and with no pity, 32 people who, knowing the judgment of God, namely, that anyone who does such things deserves death, not only do them but also join in approving those who do them.

[29] The manuscripts have various readings of this verse, mostly differences in word order. 'Fornication' was included in the manuscript tradition followed by the translators of the AV, but is not supported by the best manuscripts and does not fit in well with the rest of the vices, which clearly come under the heading of deliberate uncharitableness.

'Excess', which the AV translates as 'covetousness' and the NEB as 'rapacity', is **pleonexiâi**, which means 'trying to have more than one should', hence 'greediness' or 'ambition'. But it covers any activity which could be described as 'going over the top', in other words, 'outrageous behaviour'. See my notes on Col. 3.5 in *Reading through Colossians and Ephesians*.

'Malice', **kakiâi**, not just 'evil'. It is associated with angry behaviour and verbal abuse in Eph. 4.31 and Col. 3.8.

'Spitefulness', **kakoêtheiâs**, literally, 'bad disposition'. It is particularly used to describe the behaviour of those who put the worst construction on everything.

'Whispering slander', **psithyristâs**, a nice example of onomatopoeia.

[30] 'Spreading evil stories', **katalalous**, i.e. 'speaking evil'.

'Hating God', **theostygeis**, AV 'haters of God', but it could be 'hateful *to* God', the usual meaning of this word and the one given by the NEB. I prefer 'hating God', however, even though it is not the usual sense, because Clement of Rome clearly took it in this sense when he re-worked this passage using abstract nouns (I Clem. 35.5) and substituted for the adjective the noun **theostygiân**, which can only mean 'hatred of God', i.e. hatred directed towards God. The Vulgate, however, has *Deo odibiles*, which can only be taken as 'hateful to God'.

'Wantonly violent', **hybristâs**, from **hybris**, which is a more active misdemeanour than the use of this word in English would suggest. In legal terminology any serious injury inflicted on a person is described as **hybris**. Paul uses the word in referring to the damages sustained during the storm off Crete on his voyage to Italy (Acts 27.21).

'Impostors', **alazonas**, is more accurate than the NEB 'boastful', since the word is often used to denote charlatans or quacks who make false pretensions.

'With no obedience', **apeitheis**. This is the first of a series of words starting with **a-** and translated here with 'no'.

[31] The juxtaposition of 'with no understanding', **asynetous**, and 'with no intention of keeping their word', **asynthetous**, is a deliberate play on words. The latter term is derived from the verb **syntithemai**, 'I make a covenant', 'I agree on'.

'With no natural affection', **astorgous**, from the noun **storgê**, which denotes particularly affection between parents and children. The treatment of unwanted infants who were regularly exposed and left to die by the pagan societies of the time was regarded by the Jews as a horrible practice and a symptom of Gentile depravity.

[32] 'Knowing the judgment (**dikaiôma**) of God' at first sight would seem to apply only to renegade Jews, because of the reference to **dikaiôma**, a word used frequently in the context of the Mosaic Law to denote an 'ordinance' or 'rule', as in 2.26 and Heb. 9.1 and 10. It is clear, however, that Paul is describing the pagans as knowing what is right and wrong, and hence as responsible for their wicked actions. Ignorance of the *Torah* is no excuse.

'Join in approving those who do them' does not necessarily refer to those who enjoy graphic depictions in literature or certain scenes in comedy and mime, as Käsemann and others suggest. It is more likely that Paul is referring in general terms to the immorality of those who not only commit crimes but encourage others to do the same.

Chapter 2

1 Therefore you are without excuse, every one of you human beings who sit in judgment. For in judging another, you condemn yourself; for you who judge do the same things. 2 We know that God's judgment on those who do such things is in accordance with truth. 3 Do you reckon, you human being judging those who do such things, and doing such things yourself, that you will escape the judgment of God? 4 Or do you despise the riches of his kindness, forbearance and patience, unaware of the fact that the kindness of God brings you to repentance? 5 Following your hardness and unrepentant heart you are piling up for yourself a treasure of anger on the day of anger and of the revelation of the righteous judgment of God,

[1] Paul suddenly changes tack in his argument. Up to now he has been attacking pagan immorality, and the Jews in his audience would have been agreeing with him. One can imagine them saying, 'Exactly, that is what happens when people turn away from the true God. Thank heavens we are not like that.' Now he tells his audience that they, too, are sinners, precisely because they 'judge', i.e. disapprove of, such immorality and yet are guilty of it. This argument seems to be directed specifically at the Jewish elements of his audience,

although it can apply also to those Gentiles who had been proselytes. Paul is pointing out that Jews do not have a privileged position in regard to the judgment of God, nor can they presume on the goodness of God. 'For there is no respect of persons with God', as Paul reminds them in v. 11. This same point is made by Justin Martyr (*Dialogue with Trypho*, 140.2) when he attacks his Jewish adversaries for believing that 'those who are the seed of Abraham according to the flesh, even if they are sinners, unbelievers (**apistoi**) and disobedient (**apeitheis**) towards God, shall in every case be granted the eternal kingdom.'

'Every one of you human beings who sit in judgment', literally, 'o, man, every judging [one]', **ô anthrôpe pâs ho krînôn.**

The second sentence is more pointed in Greek since the verbs 'I condemn', **katakrînô**, and 'I judge', **krînô**, are related.

[2] 'In accordance with truth', in other words, 'just' or 'fair'. See the note below on 'truth' in v. 8.

[3] 'You human being judging', **ô anthrôpe ho krînôn**, recalls the phrase in v. 1.

[4] 'Riches', **ploutou**; see note on 10.12.

'Kindness', **chrêstotêtos**, in the NT does not carry the derogatory sense of 'soft-heartedness' or 'naivety' which it can have in classical literature.

'Patience' or 'long-suffering', **makrothûmiâs**, occurs together with 'kindness' in Col. 3.12 in a list of virtues to be practised by Christians. There is an interesting connection between this verse and Wisdom 15.1 (Sept.), which comes after a list of pagan iniquities and says, 'But you, our God, are *kind* (**chrêstos**) and true, *long-suffering* (**makrothûmos**) and managing everything with mercy.'

'The kindness of God brings you *to repentance* (**eis**

metanoian)' can be paraphrased, 'God is kind to you when you sin because he is giving you time to repent.' Wisdom again provides a parallel (11.23), 'You have mercy on everyone, because you can [do] everything, and you overlook the sins of human beings *for repentance* (**eis metanoian**).'

[5] 'You are piling up . . . a treasure', **thêsaurizeis**, is a paradox; their 'treasure' is condemnation.

Note the repetition of 'anger'. See the note on 1.18.

'Righteous judgment', **dikaiokrisiâs**, a word found nowhere else in the NT. As Sanday and Headlam point out, it denotes not so much the character of the judgment as the character of the Judge.

6 who 'will pay back each one according to his deeds', 7 eternal life to those who by persevering in doing good seek glory, honour and immortality, 8 and anger and wrath to those who in their intrigues distrust the truth and trust injustice. 9 [There will be] tribulation and suffering for every human soul who does evil, the Jew first, and [then] also the Greek, 10 but glory, honour and peace to everyone who does good, to the Jew first, and [then] also the Greek. 11 For there is no partiality with God.

[6] The quotation seems to be a conflation of Ps. 62.12 (Sept. 61.13) and Prov. 24.12, where the former has 'you *will pay back*', and the latter '*who* pays back'.

[7] 'By persevering in doing good', literally, 'according to patience of good deed'.

[8] 'Anger and wrath', **orgê kai thûmos**, are virtually synonyms here. This is the only example in Paul's letters of

thûmos being used to denote the anger of God. In Revelation, however, it is very common. In Rev. 16.19 and 19.15 it is also used, as here, with **orgê**. It is interesting that both terms are also used in lists of vices, such as Eph. 4.31 and Col. 3.8, where I translate them as 'bad temper and anger'. Paul is making the subtle point that, just as those who seek immortality are paid back with eternal life, those who display bad temper and anger are repaid in their own coin. Incidentally, Paul's grammar goes astray, since, strictly speaking, the nouns 'anger and wrath' should have been in the accusative case, not the nominative, like the noun 'life' in the previous verse.

'In their intrigues', **ex erîtheiâs**, literally, 'out of intrigue', refers to selfish ambition exhibited by those who trample on others in their pursuit of money or status. The word originally denoted canvassing for a public office. See my notes in *Reading through Galatians* on Gal. 5.20, where the term occurs in association with 'anger', **thûmoi**.

'Distrust', **apeithousi**, and 'trust', **peithomenois**, are etymologically related. The latter can also mean 'follow', 'obey' and 'rely on'.

'Truth' here is clearly a synonym for 'justice' or 'righteousness', in other words, 'true judgment'. The association of truth and righteousness can be seen in Eph. 4.24, 'in the righteousness and holiness of truth', and in Eph. 5.9, 'in every [form of] goodness, righteousness and truth'. In the well-known verse I Cor. 13.6, '[love] does not take pleasure in the wrong, but rejoices at the truth', 'truth' is contrasted with 'wrong', **adikia**, literally, 'injustice'. John 3.21 even speaks of 'doing' the truth, and in II John 4 and III John 3 and 4 we have 'walking in' the truth. Clearly **alêtheia**, the word we translate as 'truth', has a broader sense in the NT than our word; God's **alêtheia** includes his reliability and his righteousness, and indeed his authenticity; it is not just 'telling the truth'.

[9] As I point out in my introduction to *Reading through Galatians*, Paul never contrasts faith with works as though they were diametrically opposed to each other. Good works meet with God's approval and bad works his disapproval, as this and the next verse clearly state, but that does not contradict Paul's central message that we cannot *earn* God's favour simply by good works. As he says in Eph. 2.8, 9, 'For you have been saved by grace through faith; and this [does] not [come] from you [but is] a gift of God; [it does] not [come] from works, lest anyone should boast.' There is, incidentally, no main verb in the original, but it is not uncommon in Greek to omit the verb 'to be'.

'Tribulation', **thlîpsis**, literally 'pressure', 'crushing', is often used to describe active oppression at the hands of another, i.e. persecution, as in Heb. 10.33, where I translate it as 'oppression', while 'suffering', **stenochôriâ**, literally 'narrowness of space', usually denotes difficulties caused by straitened circumstances.

'The Jew first' seems odd when we read in v. 11 that there is no partiality with God, but Paul is making the point that, because the Jews were first to receive the promises of God and privileged in being chosen by him, so they are first in line to be judged. But they still face judgment along with the rest of mankind.

'The Greek': see note on 1.16.

[10] 'Peace' is connected with the sabbath which awaits the faithful at the last day. See Heb. 4.7–11 and my notes on that passage in *Reading through Hebrews*.

[11] 'Partiality', **prosôpolêmpsiâ**, occurs also in Eph. 6.9 and Col. 3.25. See my notes on the latter passage and on Gal. 2.6 in the relevant books in this series.

12 For all those who have sinned without the Law

shall also perish without the Law, and all those who have sinned under the Law shall be judged through the Law. 13 For [it is] not the hearers of the Law [who will be] righteous before God, but the doers of the Law [who] will be justified. 14 For when Gentiles who do not have the Law naturally do what the Law stipulates, they are the Law to themselves although they do not have the Law, 15 being people who show that they have the work of the Law written on their hearts, when their conscience bears witness with them and their thoughts among one another accuse or indeed speak in their defence, 16 on the day when God judges the secrets of human beings according to my gospel through Jesus Christ.

[12] 'Without the Law', **anomôs**, literally, 'lawlessly'.

'Under the Law', **en nomôi**, literally, 'in Law'.

The main point Paul is making here is that both Gentiles and Jews face judgment, whether they ostensibly observe the *Torah* or not. He is not talking about moral codes in general, nor whether the absence of a moral code makes a difference when judging a person, but the relevance of the Mosaic Law. Jerome takes the 'Law' here as the 'law of nature', but the fact that in v. 14 the Gentiles are described as not having the 'Law' proves that 'Law' here is the *Torah*.

[13] Note that the verb 'will be justified', **dikaiôthêsontai**, here clearly is a synonym for '[will be] righteous', **dikaioi**. Note also the legal context in which these terms operate.

The sub-text of this verse is that since only those who keep the Law are justified, and since no one keeps the Law, all are guilty before God. As Paul makes clear in Gal. 3.10–12, 'everyone who does not abide by all the things written in the book of the Law and do them is accursed. It is clear that no one is justified by the Law in God's view, because "the just through faith shall live". And the Law is not of faith but "he who has done them shall live by them".' Paul will, of course, go on to spell this out in the next chapter.

[14] Does 'naturally', **physei**, go with the previous or the following clause? The AV, 'do by nature the things contained in the law', and the Moffatt version, 'obey instinctively the Law's requirements', support the latter, but I have deliberately left it, as it is in Greek, in an ambiguous position. I believe, however, that it goes with the previous clause and we should translate it as 'who do not *by nature* have the Law'. The same word is used in Gal. 2.15, 'We are Jews *by nature* and not Gentile sinners', to refer to the fact that Paul and Peter were born and bred as Jews. This is better than taking 'naturally' with the following clause, since that would imply that some people are natural observers of the Mosaic Law (presumably blessed with a law-abiding gene). Paul is talking about the relative status of Jews and Gentiles, not the difference between those who are naturally inclined to keep the Law and those who find it difficult.

'What the Law stipulates', **ta tou nomou**, literally, 'the [things] of the Law'.

'They are *the* Law to themselves', not, as the AV has it, 'these . . . are a law unto themselves'. Aristotle (*Nicomachean Ethics*, 1128a, 31) describes the 'refined gentleman' as 'being like a law to himself', **hoion nomos ôn heautôi**, because he shows restraint in the sort of jokes that he makes and avoids offending others. In other words, he voluntarily adopts a code of practice which is not necessarily a legal requirement. Some commentators assume that Paul is referring to something like 'the natural law' of the Stoics from which they derived the principles of natural justice, but Käsemann, while I believe he is wrong to take **physei** with the clause 'do what the Law

stipulates', is right to recommend caution in regard to this
assumption. Paul is only concerned here with the Law
revealed in scripture and would in any case have argued that
the 'natural law' was merely a pale reflection of the *Torah*.
The absence of a definite article in Paul's Greek, as I point out
in my notes on Gal. 2.16 in *Reading through Galatians*, is
common, and cannot be used as proof that he is not referring
to *the* Law. 'The Law' is frequently referred to as 'Law'; for
example, in verses 12 and 13 the definite article is not used
once with 'Law', and in this verse it is only used once. Paul is
saying that Gentiles have to act as their own *Torah*, since they
do not have it, being outside the covenant.

[15] 'The work of the Law', i.e. observance of the Mosaic
Law. Gentiles reveal that they are aware of the Law and its
demands because their conscience tells them whether they
have observed the Law. Paul is probably thinking of the
observance of the major commandments, such as those
against murder or theft rather than the dietary laws.

'Among one another', **metaxy allêlôn**, is a difficult phrase;
the AV separates **metaxy** from **allêlôn** and translates **metaxy**
as 'the meanwhile', and makes 'one another' the object of the
verbs 'accusing' and 'excusing'. The Rheims version of 1582
has 'among themselves mutually', which is obviously influ-
enced by the Vulg. *inter se invicem*, but it is not clear whether
'themselves' refers to the people or to their thoughts. The
NEB is close to the meaning with 'their own thoughts argue
the case *on either side*, against them or even for them'. The
idea seems to be that in the human mind there are, as it were,
two sides, a prosecutor and a defence lawyer arguing *between
themselves* about the guilt or innocence of the defendant.
Jerome certainly interprets the passage this way, 'He (Paul) is
speaking of the quarrels between our thoughts, when we
decide in the course of our daily deliberations what we should
or should not do, and, following this, we are to be judged on

the day of the Lord . . . our conscience and our thoughts will be before our eyes on the day of judgment, like histories to be discovered, and they will either accuse us or excuse us themselves.'

[16] Some commentators, such as Barclay and Dodd place this verse between vv. 13 and 14; others would amend or exclude it altogether, but there is no reason for questioning a text which, apart from very minor variations, is well established in the manuscripts. Wanting to improve Paul's rambling and disjointed style, or his theology, is not a sufficient reason for such drastic alteration. Furthermore, it makes perfectly good sense to set the consciousness of guilt in the context of the final judgment day. As Käsemann says, 'this reference to the judgment is indispensable.'

'According to my gospel through Jesus Christ', not 'by Jesus Christ according to my gospel', as the AV has it, or the NEB, which has as a final sentence, 'So my gospel declares.' The phrase 'through Jesus Christ' should not be taken with 'judges'. Paul is referring to the fact that his gospel came to him from Christ himself and so he has good authority for what he has just said. He is reminding his audience that final judgment is included in the gospel message delivered by Christ himself.

17 And if you are called a Jew and rest upon the Law and boast of God, 18 and [if] you know [his] will and approve of the things that matter, receiving instruction from the Law, 19 and [if] you believe yourself to be a guide to the blind, a light to those in darkness, 20 an instructor of the foolish, a teacher of children, with your appearance of knowledge and truth in the Law – 21 well, then, you who teach others, don't you teach yourself? You who preach against theft, do you steal?

22 You who tell [people] not to commit adultery, do
you commit adultery? You who abominate idols, do
you commit sacrilege?

[17] 'And if', **ei de**, appears in later manuscripts as **ide**,
'behold', which is the reading we find in the AV. The reason
for the corrupt reading is the fact that in later Greek it had the
same pronunciation.

'Rest upon', **epanapauêi**, is only found in one other place
in the NT, Luke 10.6, which, referring to the salutation
'peace be to this house', says, 'and if the Son of Peace is there,
your "peace" *will rest upon* it'. Clearly the word also carries
the sense of 'abide in' or 'stay firmly placed on'. Jerome
glosses this word as *confidis vel securus es*, 'trust in or are
confident'.

'Boast of God' can be paraphrased as 'tell everyone how
proud you are to be privileged to serve the one true God'.
'Boast' does not necessarily carry a bad sense, as we can see
from the way it is used by Paul, e.g. Gal. 6.4 and 14.

[18] 'Approve', **dokimazeis**, a verb which usually means 'test'
or 'examine', as in Eph. 5.10, but here, as in Gal. 6.4, implies
'pass as correct after examination'.

'The things that matter', **ta diapheronta**, from the verb
diapherô, 'I differ', which used impersonally in the third
person means 'it makes a difference', hence 'it matters'. The
expression could also mean 'the things that stand out as
excellent', hence the AV has 'the things that are more
excellent', and the Vulgate has *utiliora*, 'the things that are
more useful'. The expression 'approve of the things that
matter' occurs also in Phil. 1.10, but we cannot tell from the
context of that verse either whether **ta diapheronta** should be
taken as meaning 'the things that matter' or 'the things that
stand out as excellent'. I prefer the former because moral
philosophers of the period used the opposite term **ta adia-**

phora to denote 'the things that are neither good nor bad'. So **ta diapheronta** must denote 'matters of moral concern' or 'morality'. The NEB has 'you *are aware* of moral distinctions' (1961 edition) and 'you *know* right from wrong' (1970 edition), but Paul is saying of the Jew not that he knows the difference between right and wrong but that he claims to approve of the former.

'Receiving instruction', **katêchoumenos**, from which we derive 'catechumen'.

[19] This verse echoes Isa. 42.6, 7 (AV), '. . . for *a light* of the Gentiles; to open the *blind* eyes, to bring out the prisoners from the prison, and them that sit *in darkness* out of the prison house.'

[20] 'Children', **nêpiôn**, rather than 'infants' or 'the childish' here. Jerome takes it as referring either to actual children or those who are like children, *aetate vel sensu*, 'either in age or in intelligence'.

'With your appearance', **echonta tên morphôsin**, literally, 'having the form'. Compare II Tim. 3.5, the only other place in the NT where the word **morphôsis** occurs, 'having the appearance of piety, but denying its power'. Lightfoot suggests that this word means a rough sketch or an outline without the substance.

'Knowledge and truth in the Law' is virtually the same as 'true knowledge of the Law'.

[21] Typically of Paul, this is a new sentence interrupting the previous conditional sentence before its main clause is reached. Note also that we would have expected Paul to follow 'don't you teach yourself?' with further questions in the negative, i.e. '*don't* you steal . . . *don't* you commit adultery . . . *don't* you commit sacrilege?', but good style is not one of his priorities.

[22] 'Commit sacrilege', **hierosûleis**, literally, 'rob temples'. It may seem unlikely that a Jew who claimed to obey the Law would 'commit sacrilege', but the crime would cover the kind of commercial transaction which provoked Jesus in the Temple when he overturned the tables of the money changers. Käsemann suggests that the literal meaning 'rob temples' is what is intended here and that Paul is referring to such things as handling property stolen from pagan temples. This is certainly preferable to interpreting the expression figuratively or metaphorically, as Barrett does when he suggests that the Jew who loathes idolatry can commit sacrilege himself, 'but when he exalts himself as judge and lord over his fellow-creatures he renders this devotion to – himself!' It is interesting that Philo (*On The Confusion of Languages*, 163) also mentions together, and in the same order, 'stealing', 'committing adultery' and 'committing sacrilege', but he also includes 'committing murder'.

23 You, who boast of the Law, dishonour God by breaking the Law; 24 for, as it is written, 'the name of God because of you is blasphemed among the Gentiles'. 25 For, to be sure, circumcision is an advantage if you keep the Law; but if are a law breaker, your circumcision has become an uncircumcision. 26 So if the uncircumcised safeguards the decrees of the Law, surely his lack of circumcision will be reckoned as circumcision, 27 and his physical lack of circumcision, by fulfilling the Law, will judge you the transgressor of the Law in the letter and in your circumcision? 28 For he is not a Jew who is visibly one, nor is his visible and fleshly circumcision [a real circumcision], 29 but he is a Jew who is one in secret, and whose circumcision is of the heart in the spirit

and not in the letter, and his praise [is] not from men but from God.

[23–29] This passage tends to be seen as expressing a particular doctrine of Paul, which will be explored fully later, namely, that the faithful Gentile who believes in Christ is a true Israelite and has fulfilled the Law more perfectly than the Jew whose religion is formal and external and not based on a real spiritual foundation. This is the teaching we find in Gal. 6.16, where the 'Israel of God' are the true people of God rather than those who call themselves Israelites, and in Col. 2.11, where the spiritual circumcision of the Gentile believer is described, 'And it is in him that you were circumcised with a circumcision not done by hands, but in the stripping off of the body of flesh in Christ's circumcision', a statement explained in the following verses by being set in the context of baptism. Paul, however, is not focussing here on the status of the Christian Gentile but on the validity of circumcision in the case of the Jew who fails to keep the Law and on the question of how to define a true Jew.

[23] The AV treats this verse as a question, but I follow Käsemann and Sanday and Headlam in treating it as a statement which sums up the previous argument and links with the next section.

'Dishonour God' is explained by Chrysostom as 'they (the Jews) dishonour him (God) who honoured them'.

[24] The quotation is from Isa. 52.5 (Sept.), 'Because my people have been taken away for nothing, be amazed and howl (thus says the Lord). Because of you my name is continually blasphemed among the Gentiles.' Ezekiel 36.20 is similar, but not close enough in phrasing and language. The original Hebrew version of the Isaiah passage seems to

attribute the blaspheming to the Israelites, not the Gentiles, as we can see when we compare the AV, 'they that rule over them make them to howl, saith the Lord; and my name continually every day is blasphemed'. The blaspheming by the Gentiles to which Paul refers presumably consists in making disparaging remarks about the God of the Jews, such as, 'What kind of God is this whose people behave so badly?' The Sept. version implies that the Gentiles criticized the God of the Jews for a different reason. In other words they would say, 'What kind of God is this who fails to protect his people?' This use of a text to extract another meaning than the one originally intended is perfectly valid and typical of rabbinical argument.

[25] The key word here is the first 'if'. As he argues elsewhere, no one can keep the Law, and therefore the condition is not met. By breaking the Law the Jew's circumcision is rendered invalid because he has not kept the covenant of which his circumcision is a badge; it is as though he was never circumcised.

'Keep' is literally 'do', **prassêis**.

[26] This is a subtle argument which could be interpreted in several ways. Firstly, we can take it at its face value as saying that by fulfilling the Law a righteous Gentile is a better Jew than a Jew who does not observe the Law. Secondly, we can take it hypothetically, and argue that if a Gentile *were to* keep the Law, he *would* be an honorary Jew, but, of course, no one can keep the Law, and so he, too, is outside the covenant. Thirdly, we can argue that the Christian Gentile is reckoned as circumcised because he is allowed to become one of the people of God through faith in Christ. Such a one is an heir to the promises given to Abraham and a true Israelite. In a sense, therefore, a Gentile can 'safeguard the decrees of the Law'. As I have already said, I believe that Paul at this stage is more

interested in the status of the Jew who, while he claims to rely on the *Torah*, fails to keep its commandments, than the status of the Gentile Christian who relies on faith in Christ, nor is he arguing here that all human beings have sinned (that comes later). I would, therefore, favour the first interpretation as being the most relevant for this passage and assume *for the sake of the argument* that there is such a person as the non-Jew who keeps the Law.

'The decrees', **ta dikaiômata**, are the individual ordinances and rules which constitute the Mosaic Law. They seem to be identical with **ta dogmata** of Eph. 2.15, which correspond to the Hebrew term *mitzvot*. See my notes on that verse in *Reading through Colossians and Ephesians*.

[27] 'Physical', **ek physeos**, literally, 'from nature'.

'Judge', i.e. 'condemn', because the righteous Gentile provides the standard by which the Jew who fails to fulfil the Law will be found guilty.

'In the letter and in your circumcision' must be taken as qualifying the noun 'transgressor' because of the Greek word order, i.e. 'you the-through the letter and circumcision-transgressor of the Law'. It cannot be treated as a phrase qualifying the verb 'will judge'. Hence the NEB 'he will pass judgment on you who break it, *for all your written code and your circumcision*' cannot be right. The AV 'thee, who by the letter and circumcision dost transgress the law' and the Vulg. *te qui per litteram et circumcisionem praevaricator legis es* are correct. Paul is saying in effect, 'you will be condemned as a transgressor *by the criteria of* the code *you claim to* follow as a circumcised Jew'; he is not saying, 'you will be condemned as a transgressor, *despite* the code you follow as a circumcised Jew'.

[28–29] The meaning of these verses is that a real Jew is not one because he is physically circumcised but because he is spiritually circumcised. Hence he is more interested in pleasing God than men. Paul is preparing the ground for defining the nature of spiritual circumcision, a subject which will be explored in chapter 4 in reference to Abraham.

'Praise', **epainos**, according to some commentators, is a punning reference either to the word for 'Jew' or to the Hebrew name Judah, both of which are traditionally supposed to mean 'praise' (see Gen. 29.35 and 49.8). Barrett tries to reproduce this pun in English, 'He is a Jew, whose *due* comes not from men but from God.' So the last part of v. 29 has another meaning, i.e. true Jewishness comes from God, not men. The connection is clearer in Greek: Judah/**Ioudas**, Jew/**Ioudaios**. There might also be a reference to the fact that Jesus was of the tribe of Judah (see Heb. 7.14 and 8.8).

Chapter 3

1 So what advantage does the Jew have, or what is the use of circumcision? 2 A great deal in every way. Principally because they were entrusted with the words of God. 3 But what if some of them were unfaithful? Surely their faithlessness will not nullify God's faithfulness? 4 God forbid! Let God be true and every human being false, as it is written, 'so that you may be justified in your words and prevail in your judgment'. 5 And if our unrighteousness establishes God's righteousness, what shall we say? Surely God is not unjust because he brings retribution [upon us]? (I am speaking in the way that people do) 6. God forbid! for [if he is unjust,] how will he judge the world?

[1] This verse is the first of a series of questions Paul puts into the mouth of an imagined opponent. The passage is not easy to follow and Dodd calls the whole argument of vv. 1–8 'obscure and feeble', adding, 'When Paul, who is normally a clear as well as a forcible thinker, becomes feeble and obscure, it usually means that he is defending a poor case . . . The argument of the epistle would go much better if this whole section were omitted.' One can sympathize with Dodd's frustration, but it could be that he misunderstands what Paul is actually saying. Paul can sometimes leave out steps in his

argument or use a tortuous syntax when he is excited or when his mind is moving faster than his speech. Chapter 2 of Galatians provides several examples of this characteristic.

'Advantage', **perisson**, literally, 'extraordinary', 'remarkable'. It is the root of **perisseuô**, 'I overflow', 'I abound', a favourite verb of Paul, which he uses in v. 7. **Perisson** is found in John 10.10 (AV), 'I am come that they might have life, and that they might have it *more abundantly*.'

[2] Paul answers by agreeing with the implicit assumption behind his opponent's question, namely, that Jews did have a privileged position compared with Gentiles, but a privileged position which has to be strictly defined.

'Principally,' rather than 'firstly', the usual translation of **prôton**, because there is no 'secondly' following.

'Words', **ta logia**, literally, 'the sayings', Vulg. *eloquia*. It is odd that so many modern versions such as the NEB keep the AV's 'oracles' as a translation of this word, giving it a bias which it does not have in the original. Robinson, who also translates **ta logia** as 'the oracles', thinks that they are the 'promises', but that is far too narrow a definition, and completely distorts Paul's argument. **Ta logia** are the revelations of God's will as recorded in the scriptures, particularly on those occasions when God speaks directly to human beings, e.g. the Law given to Moses by God on Sinai. 'Oracles', on the other hand, are generally cryptic answers given to devotees who have come to a shrine to pose questions to the divinity who is thought to reside there. The distinguishing feature of most of these 'oracular' replies is that they require interpretation. A typical example would be those oracles given at the Pythian shrine in Delphi, which were intended to mystify. See my note on Heb. 5.12 regarding **ta logia tou Theou** in *Reading through Hebrews*.

The fact that the Jews were chosen by God to receive the scriptures and the Law is central to Paul's argument, since he will use those same scriptures to convince his opponents that the old covenant has been superseded, and that the promises given to Abraham are not dependent on the Mosaic Law.

[3] The argument at this point is rather abbreviated and we need to flesh it out a little. Paul's opponent now argues something like this: 'You say that Jews have been unfaithful and have broken the Law. So what if they have? Surely it does not follow that God has broken faith and cancelled the covenant?' There is, incidentally, a play on words here which depends on the fact that the word which I translate as 'faithfulness', namely **pistis**, is the common root in the words 'unfaithful' and 'faithlessness', and 'were entrusted' in the previous verse. This word will appear again eighteen times between here and the end of the next chapter. As I point out in my notes on Gal. 3.9, **pistis**, like the adjective **pistos**, has a wider range of meanings than any single equivalent word in English. It is intellectual 'belief' and emotional 'trust', active 'trustfulness' and passive 'trustworthiness'. When applied to God, as it is here, it refers to his 'trustworthiness', the fact that he keeps his promises.

'Surely . . . not', **mê**, Vulg. *numquid*, makes this into a question expecting the answer 'of course not'. The AV misses this loading of the question.

'Will . . . nullify', **katargêsei**, a legal term used almost exclusively by Paul in the NT. It occurs in a passage in Galatians (3.17) which makes the point that the promises given to Abraham were not made invalid by the Mosaic Law. In Eph. 2.15 it is used to describe the action of Christ '*having abolished* (**katargêsâs**) the Law of the command-ments'.

[4] The quotation is from Ps. 50.6 (Sept.), which corresponds to Ps. 51.4 in the AV (the different numbering is due to the fact that the Septuagint combines the two Hebrew psalms 9

and 10 into one, affecting the numbering of the subsequent
psalms, while the individual verses also are often divided
differently). The context of the quotation is a plea by the
psalmist for forgiveness and an acknowledgment that, when
he is faced with the judgment of God, he is guilty, God's
sentence against him is justified, and God is right in winning
his case against him.

'Let God be true', literally, 'let God *become* (**gînesthô**)
true', i.e. 'may it be revealed that God is true'.

[5] The objector now opens with a parody of Paul's teaching
which Paul will attack in the next verse, 'If our sin gives God
an opportunity to demonstrate his righteousness, in other
words, our sin is necessary to enable God to be righteous,
surely he cannot be so unjust as to punish us for a sin which he
has engineered?' This last remark is such an outrageous thing
to suggest that Paul, or his opponent, feels he has to insert a
note of apology – 'I'm only quoting what people might say',
literally, 'I speak according to a human being', i.e. 'I speak in
human terms'. Jerome explains it as meaning 'according to
you who think like this'.

'Establishes', **synistêsin**, which can also be translated 'con-
trives', 'guarantees', 'demonstrates' or 'recommends'. The last
meaning seems to be the one preferred by the Vulg. *commen-
dat*, from which the AV derived 'commend'.

'Retribution', **orgên**, literally, 'anger'. See note on 1.18.

[6] I have inserted the suppressed conditional clause to make
the meaning clear. This is a rhetorical question: Paul is
arguing from the fact that God will judge the world (**kosmon**,
which can also mean 'everybody') to the conclusion that he
must be just; he is not really contemplating the possibility that
God could be unjust. This recalls the question posed by
Abraham in Gen.18.25 (Sept.), 'You who judge the whole
earth, will you not make judgment?'

7 But if the truth of God was made to overflow to his glory by my falsehood, why am I also still judged as [being] a sinner? 8 Surely we are not to do evil so that good may come [of it] (as we are falsely accused of saying, as some people allege, and their condemnation is just)?

[7, 8] These two verses are so abbreviated and complicated that the meaning is difficult to extract. Paul's emotional involvement can be seen from the way he interrupts the argument with an indignant reminder that he has been falsely accused of telling people that they can sin with impunity. The objector develops his previous point, 'If sin is necessary for God's righteousness to operate, leaving aside the injustice of being found guilty in the first place, why does God continue ('still') to treat us as actual sinners? You imply that sin is good because it increases God's righteousness, but surely we should not do evil in order that good might come of it?'

'Truth', as I point out in my notes on 2.8, is a synonym for 'righteousness', and so 'falsehood' must be a synonym for 'unrighteousness' or 'wickedness'.

'Surely . . . not', **mê**. As in v. 3, the negative tends to be ignored by translators. My parentheses have tidied up the shape of the sentence, but Paul actually interrupts twice: firstly, with the complaint that he has been falsely accused of encouraging people to sin, and secondly, with the remark that 'they' deserve condemnation. This could be taken as referring to people who say we should sin, but it probably refers to Paul's slanderers. At his first interruption he drags the verb 'let us do', which is needed to complete the main sentence, into his complaint, 'they say that we say "let us do evil"'. To give some idea of the problems involved in translating this verse, here is the most literal version: 'And not as we are slandered and as some say that we say that we are to do the evil so that there may come the good? Of whom the judgment is right.'

9 What then? Are we in a worse position? Not at all. For we previously accused both Jews and Greeks of all being under sin, 10 as it is written, 'There is no one just, no, not one; 11 there is no one who understands, no one who seeks God. 12 All have turned aside, and been corrupted alike. There is no one who does good; there is no one, not even one. 13 Their throat is an opened grave. They have dealt treacherously with their tongues; asp venom is under their lips, 14 and their mouths are full of cursing and bitterness. 15 Their feet are quick to shed blood; 16 ruin and wretchedness are in their ways, 17 and they have not known the way of peace. 18 There is no fear of God before their eyes.'

[9] 'Are we in a worse position', **proëchometha**, literally, 'are we excelled', is the best manuscript reading. The AV 'are we better than they' and the Vulg. *praecellimus* are based on a different reading. Some commentators recognize that **proëchometha** is the best reading but translate it as 'are we in a *better* position', as though this verb were in the middle voice with the same sense as the active form of the verb, **proëchomen**, 'we excel'. (Remember that the middle corresponds to the deponent verb in Latin, which has an active meaning although it looks passive.) The passive sense of this verb, i.e. 'we are excelled', however, is common, while the middle seems only to allow the meaning 'we put forward as a pretext'. Apart from the fact that the translation 'are we in a worse position' is grammatically correct, it also makes better sense. Paul's opponent now can be paraphrased as saying,

'You say that we Jews are not at an advantage. Are we then at a disadvantage compared with the Gentiles?' Incidentally, the NEB gives both translations, one of them in a footnote.

'We previously accused', i.e. in the first two chapters.

[10] Paul, in a typically rabbinical way, starts to quote a series of texts which have been strung together to prove that all human beings have sinned and are guilty before God. It is not clear where we should look for the source of this one, but Eccl. 7.20, 'there is no just human being on earth', is the closest parallel. Incidentally, the series of texts from vv. 13 to 18 was wrongly inserted into Ps. 14, where it persisted for many years. The Psalter of the Book of Common Prayer continued to give this inflated version of the psalm until 1928.

[11] This comes from Ps. 14. 2 (Sept. 13.2), slightly altered from the original, which reads, 'The Lord looked out from heaven over the sons of men to see if there was *anyone who understood, or who sought God.*'

[12] This continues from the previous verse and is virtually identical with the original.

[13] Paul now turns to Ps. 5.9 (Sept. 5.10) for the first two statements; the reference to 'asp venom' comes from Ps. 140.3 (Sept. 139.4).

'Opened', rather than the usual 'open', is a more accurate translation of **aneôigmenos**. An open grave could be newly dug awaiting a burial; an open*ed* grave exposing a decaying body is a far more horrific image.

[14] This is from Ps. 10.7 (Sept. 9.28), with the original 'his' now reading 'their'. The word order has also been changed and the original reference to 'deceit', **dolou**, omitted to avoid

repetition since it is the root of 'dealt treacherously', **edoliou-san**, in the previous verse.

[15–17] The quotation is from Isa. 59.7, 8. The vocabulary is not identical and there are several omissions.

[18] Paul ends his series of quotations with Ps. 36.1 (Sept. 35.2), again changing 'his' to 'their'.

19 We know that what the Law says, it says to those under the Law, so that every mouth may be stopped and so that the whole world may face trial before God, 20 since no flesh will be justified by the works of the Law before him, seeing that knowledge of sin [comes] through the Law.

[19] Having proved through his quotations from the Law (a term which covers all scripture, as I point out in my notes on Gal. 2.16, in *Reading through Galatians*) that all men are guilty before God, Paul tells his audience that those under the Law, i.e. Jews, cannot say anything in their defence, faced with the Law he has quoted, and that the 'whole world', i.e. Gentiles as well, face trial before God for their sin.

[20] 'No flesh will be justified by the works of the Law', literally, 'all flesh will not be justified', is repeated in Gal. 2.16. See my notes on that verse. The only thing the Law has done has been to convict mankind of sin; it has defined what is right and wrong, and because mankind is incapable of keeping its requirements, shown them to be 'unrighteous', i.e. 'unjustified'. Gentiles cannot escape this guilt on the grounds that they were never required to observe the Law, since the Law has defined right and wrong for everybody, and

everybody knows what is right or wrong. This theme is dealt with in chapter 7.

21 And now, independently of the Law, the righteousness of God has been revealed, attested by the Law and the prophets, 22 the righteousness of God [which comes] through faith in Jesus Christ for all believers (for there is no distinction). 23 For all have sinned and fall short of the glory of God, 24 and are justified freely by his grace through the redemption by Christ Jesus, 25 whom God determined [should be] an expiation through faith in his blood, in order to show his righteousness, because of the remission of sins which were committed beforehand, 26 with God's forbearance in order to show his righteousness at the present time, so that he is just and justifies the [one who comes] from faith in Jesus.

[21] 'Independently of', **chôris**, i.e. 'apart from'. Paul is drawing attention to the fact that the new covenant is nothing to do with the old covenant embodied in the Mosaic Law, but that, paradoxically, it is the Law and the prophets which bear witness to this new covenant. As we shall see, and as other letters of Paul make clear, the new covenant is based on the promises made to Abraham before the Mosaic Law existed.

'Righteousness' here and in the following verses is **dikaiosynê**. The translation 'justification' is also correct. See the notes on 1.17.

'Has been revealed', **pephanerôtai**, perfect tense referring to the revelation of the new covenant through the sacrifice of Christ.

[22] 'Faith in Jesus Christ' (objective), literally, 'faith *of* Jesus

Christ', cannot be taken as meaning 'the faith manifested by Jesus Christ' (subjective). See *Reading through Galatians*, 40–1.

The sentence 'for there is no distinction' reiterates the universality of the previous passage. 'All' those who believe in Jesus, whether Jew or Gentile, are justified. In 10.12 Paul explicitly states, 'For there is no distinction between Jew and Greek.' This is underlined by the 'all' of the next verse, namely, the fact that 'all' are sinners. The AV 'unto all and upon all' is based upon the reading **eis pantas kai epi pantas**, but the best reading is simply **eis pantas**.

'Distinction', **diastolê**, is an interesting word, used in medicine and law, and even music, as we see in I Cor. 14.7. One of its meanings is 'fence', or 'boundary', and we are reminded of the barrier which separated Gentiles from Jews in the Temple which Christ symbolically destroyed when he abolished the Law (Eph. 2.14, 15).

[23] 'Fall short', **hysterountai**, from **hystereô**, the opposite of **perisseuô**, 'I overflow', which I mention in the notes on v. 1. **Hystereô** can also mean 'I lose', as in Heb. 4.1, or 'I am destitute', as in Heb. 11.37. Hence to 'fall short of the glory of God' is to be deprived of the reward of glory which God gives to the faithful in the world to come. The NEB has 'are deprived of the divine splendour'. Käsemann states that this verse does not look toward the future glory, but toward the lost glory. It is true that mankind has lost the glory which it possessed in Adam in his state of innocence before the fall, but this same glory is restored in the world to come, and Paul speaks of this coming glory on more than one occasion.

[24] 'Freely', **dôreân**, i.e. 'as a free gift', a word virtually synonymous with the phrase 'by his grace'.

'Redemption', **apolytrôseôs**, is release from captivity on the payment of a ransom. Payment is an essential component of this word. As we can see from Eph. 1.7, the payment is the blood of Christ. The NEB obscures the true meaning of this term and translates it as 'act of liberation'. See my notes on Col. 1.14 in *Reading through Colossians and Ephesians*.

[25] 'Determined', **proëtheto**, or 'put forward', a word found only in the NT in Romans and Eph. 1.9, where I translate it as 'displayed'.

'Expiation', **hîlastêrion**, only found in the NT here and in Heb. 9.5, where it denotes the Mercy Seat in the Holy of Holies. 'Propitiation' is a possible translation, but, as Robinson points out, the verb **hîlaskesthai** in the Septuagint usually takes as its object sin or something polluted by sin; it rarely has God as its object. So the idea of wiping out sin, i.e. expiation, is to be preferred to the one of appeasing an angry God, i.e. propitiation. The connection between the sacrifice of Christ and the Mercy Seat, where blood offerings for sin were made on the Day of Atonement, is made explicit in chapter 9 of the letter to the Hebrews, and is clearly intended to suggest comparison here. Origen also took the word as referring to the Mercy Seat, extracting, incidentally, a great deal of allegorical detail from the description of the material and proportions of the object in Ex. 37.6. Incidentally, **hîlastêrion** could be an adjective, 'expiatory', but that would not make much difference to the interpretation.

'Because of the remission', i.e. 'because he has remitted'.

[26] This is a difficult verse to follow because Paul has tried to cram it full of meaning. Firstly, he repeats the phrase 'in order to show his righteousness'; secondly, he makes an antithesis between the past ('sins which were committed beforehand') and 'the present time'; and thirdly, he plays on the connection between the three words **dikaiosynês**, 'righteousness', **dikaion**, 'just', and **dikaiounta**, 'justifying'. As far as one can judge, he is saying that God *has shown* how 'righteous' he is

by wiping out past sin, and *is showing* the same 'right-eousness' by continuing to wipe out the sins of those who believe in Jesus. In other words, God has wiped the slate clean and also is prepared to forgive any sins that might be committed after the great act of atonement.

Does 'with God's forbearance', literally, 'in the forbearance of God', go with v. 25 or v. 26? The AV and the NEB both place it with the previous verse, and Nestle-Aland, the Greek text that I use, places it in v. 26 while assigning it to v. 25 by punctuation. But, grammatically speaking, if we place it in v. 25, the word 'God's' is redundant since 'God' occurs at the beginning of that verse. Furthermore, there is no reason why we should not leave it in v. 26. After all, why must we assume that God's forbearance can only apply to sins that he tolerated in the past?

27 So where is the boast? It has been excluded. Through which Law? The Law of works? No, through the law of faith. 28 For we reckon that a human being is justified by faith independently of the works of the Law. 29 Is God only [the God] of the Jews? [Is he] not also [the God] of the Gentiles? Certainly [he is the God] of the Gentiles too, 30 if there is one God who will justify the circumcised [who comes] from faith and the uncircumcised through their faith. 31 So are we abolishing the Law by means of faith? God forbid! We are establishing the Law.

[27] Some manuscripts add 'your', **sou**; hence the Vulg. *Ubi est ergo gloriatio tua*? Although this reading is not the best one, it points us towards the right interpretation. Paul, as Jerome points out, *ad Iudaeum loquitur*, is addressing the

Jew, who is proud of belonging to the nation of Israel, and telling him that his privilege has come to an end; he can no longer boast of the Law. Previously he could have done so, since there was nothing in the Law that precluded boasting about the privilege of observing it. But now it is no longer possible to boast of the Mosaic Law, since it has been superseded by the new 'Law', the covenant based on faith that has come into force following the sacrifice of Christ. The statement in v. 31 that the Law is not being abolished but established does not contradict this, as we shall see. The NEB translates the first part of this verse as 'What room then is left for human pride?' and, by gratuitously introducing the word 'human', implies that *all mankind*, Jew and Gentile alike, can no longer boast of earning God's favour by good works. But the old idea that Paul is contrasting justification by *faith* with justification by *works* has been shown by such theologians as Dunn and Sanders to be a misunderstanding of Paul's doctrine. The real contrast is between the new covenant initiated by Christ's sacrifice and the old covenant represented by the keeping of the Mosaic Law, as I point out in the introduction to *Reading through Galatians* (5, 6). Paul is addressing the Jew who is proud of his observance of the Law, i.e. of performing 'the works of the Law', since in the next verse he specifically describes justification as not coming from 'the works of the Law'. Of course, he speaks in that verse of 'a human being', i.e. 'man', **anthrôpon**, being justified, but the point he is making there is that all human beings, without distinction, are now justified by faith and not by the works of the Law, not that all human beings used to boast. After all, how could the Gentiles have boasted about their observance of the Law? They were excluded from the nation of Israel.

[28] 'Independently': see note on v. 21.

[29] Paul is still addressing his Jewish objector. Having

already informed him that his special privilege as a possessor of the Law is not going to save him from judgment, he now tells him that the Jews do not have a monopoly of God. The term 'God of Israel' is doubtless uppermost in his objector's mind, and Paul is hinting at the absurdity of believing that the God of the Jews was exclusively theirs.

[30] If there is one God, there is one form of justification.

'From faith', **ek pisteôs**, contrasts with 'through their faith', **dia tês pisteôs**. Several commentators, such as Barrett, have claimed that they are merely synonyms and that no distinction is intended. Origen, however, pointed out that the use of different prepositions was deliberate, and as an example of the difference between **ek** and **dia** quoted I Cor. 11.12, 'For as the woman [comes] from (**ek**) the man, so too [does] the man [come] through (**dia**) the woman; but everything [comes] from (**ek**) God.' The distinction seems to be based on the fact that the one comes before the other. Lightfoot, while pointing out that the same contrast between these prepositions occurs in Gal. 2.16, adds, 'Faith is strictly speaking only the means, not the source, of justification. The one preposition (**dia**) excludes this latter notion, while the other (**ek**) might imply it.' Robinson says of this distinction, 'God will not justify the circumcision **ek nomou**, on the ground of the law, because they have the law, and he will not justify the uncircumcision **dia tou nomou**, by putting them through the law, i.e. by making them become Jews.' In other words, the Jews can now be justified *from* faith, not *from* the Law, and the Gentiles *through* their faith, not by being circumcised in order to come *through* the Law; all are justified alike.

[31] The apparent contradiction, to which I refer above, between what Paul has said previously and what he says in this verse, can be easily explained. He is merely echoing the thought behind Jesus' words in Matt. 5.17, 'Do not think that

I have come to destroy the Law or the prophets; I have not come to destroy but to fulfil.' The paradox of this verse is obvious: in fulfilling the spiritual principles behind the Law, the new 'Law' of faith in Jesus (v. 27) makes the 'fleshly' Law redundant. The Law is abolished and yet it is established. As Paul says in 7.12, 'the Law is holy and the commandment holy, righteous and good'; in other words, there is a spiritual aspect to the Law which cannot be superseded. As Chrysostom says, 'What was the job (**ergon**) of the Law, and for what sake were all its activities? To make a human being righteous.' This is a subject which Paul explores in chapter 7.

Some commentators cannot accept that the Law may be both abolished and established at the same time and try to explain away the paradox. For example, they define the Law in this verse as general moral law, and imagine that Paul is saying that the abolition of the Mosaic Law establishes the moral law. Dodd, on the other hand, seems to think that the Law which is being established is 'the total revelation of God in the Old Testament', and the Law which has been abolished is the 'code of commands'. He admits that Paul believed that 'the moral principles which underlie the precepts of the Law are, in fact, fulfilled by those who rely on divine grace', but then surprisingly adds, 'but it is not relevant here'.

Paul, I believe, could also be referring to the subject of the next chapter in which he will establish the validity of the Law, i.e. the scriptural account of Abraham, because it shows that the faith displayed by Abraham is identical with the faith in Christ which has saved all mankind.

Chapter 4

1 So what shall we say Abraham our forefather in the flesh has obtained? 2 For if Abraham was justified by works, he has something to boast about, but not before God. 3 For what does the scripture say? 'Abraham had faith in God, and that was put down to him as righteousness.' 4 When somebody is doing some work, his wage is not reckoned to be a favour but something that is owed to him. 5 But if someone does not do any work, but has faith in the one who justifies the sinner, his faith is put down to him as righteousness.

The subject of this chapter, Abraham, is now introduced. This is the theme on which the whole of Paul's message hinges, and which is also explored in chapter 3 of Galatians. See my notes on vv. 6–29 of that chapter in *Reading through Galatians*. It might be helpful to give a brief schema of the subtle argument of this skilfully crafted chapter of Romans:

1. Abraham was granted justification because he had faith in God, not because he had earned it by performing some meritorious deed.

2. Abraham was not circumcised at the time that he was

justified, and is, therefore, the father of the uncircumcised, i.e. the Gentiles, who have faith.

3. Abraham received circumcision as a seal of the justification by faith which he had been granted while he was still uncircumcised. Hence he is also the father of the circumcised, i.e. Jews, who have the faith which he had while he was still uncircumcised.

4. Consequently, the promises which God made to Abraham apply to those who have his faith; they do not operate through the Law.

5. Abraham believed God when he said that he would be the father of many nations, although he and Sarah were too old to have children.

6. The righteousness imputed to Abraham is also imputed to those who have faith in the God who raised Jesus from the dead.

When one compares this chapter with the corresponding section of Galatians, one can see that many of the same points are made, but in a more orderly fashion and without its highly emotional approach. There is a difference of approach, too, because in this chapter Paul is arguing that Abraham was justified through faith while he was uncircumcised, whereas in Galatians the emphasis is on the fact that Abraham was justified at a time before the Mosaic Law existed.

[1, 2] 'Forefather', **propatora**, is a better reading than **patera**, i.e. 'father', and was probably altered to the latter because it is a rare word found nowhere else in the NT or the Septuagint. The use of 'our' and 'in the flesh' shows that Paul is still addressing his fellow Jews.

'Has obtained', **heurêkenai,** is omitted in a few manuscripts and found in different places in other manuscripts, but there is no reason to doubt that it was in the original text. The usual meaning of this verb is 'find', as we see in the AV reading, hence also the Vulg. *invenisse,* but the meanings 'obtain', 'acquire' or 'gain' are also common. The NEB leaves out **heurêkenai** and gives the dubious translation, 'What, then, are we to say about Abraham?' There is a grammatical problem if we omit **heurêkenai,** since we need some verb to make sense of the sentence. Assuming that **heurêkenai** is correct, what has Abraham obtained? The implicit answer to this question might have been 'something to boast about', **kauchêma,** but this answer is ruled out because Abraham was *not* justified by works. The correct answer to the question is 'justification by faith'.

[3] This quotation from Gen. 15.6 is also used in Gal. 3.6. There are minor discrepancies, as one would expect when a writer is quoting from memory. See my notes in *Reading through Galatians.*

[4] 'A favour', **kata charin,** literally, 'according to grace'. I have discussed **charis** several times in this series; see particularly the notes on Gal. 1.3 and Heb. 12.28.

[5] Strictly speaking, this is not the antithesis to the previous verse. We would have expected Paul to have said something like: 'But as for the person who does not do any work, he has not earned a wage and can expect nothing.' That would have completed the antithesis and then Paul could have explained his allegory by reference to the case of Abraham, who was given a 'wage', i.e. 'justification', although he had not done any deed to earn it. It is typical of Paul to leave out steps in his argument in his eagerness to get to the main point. As Käsemann puts it, 'the application is mingled with the

comparison and overlaps it'. This is why the reference to justifying the sinner seems out of place.

'Sinner', **asebê**, literally, 'impious', but used frequently to mean 'disloyal' or 'disobedient'. The verb **asebeô** is often used in the sense of 'I sin against'. It is interesting that Christians were accused of being **asebeis** towards the Roman emperor.

6 This is just what David is referring to when he speaks of the blessing of the man whom God justifies independently of works: 7 'Blessed are those whose transgressions have been taken away, and whose sins have been covered over; 8 blessed is the man to whom the Lord will not ascribe sin.' 9 Is this blessing, then, over the circumcised or over the uncircumcised also? For we say, 'Abraham's faith was put down to him as righteousness.' 10 How then was it put down to him? During the time he was circumcised, or while he was uncircumcised? While he was uncircumcised, not after his circumcision.

[6] 'This is just what David is referring to when he speaks of', literally, 'As even David speaks of'. 'David', as in 11.9, often introduces a quotation from the psalms.

'Blessing', **makarismon**, not 'blessedness' (AV), nor 'happiness' (NEB). As in Gal. 4.15, this Greek word is frequently mistranslated; it means, as Sanday and Headlam observe, 'pronouncing someone happy', not the state of happiness itself. The Vulg. *beatitudinem* again seems to be the cause of the misunderstanding.

'Whom God justifies', literally, 'to whom God *reckons* (**logizetai**) righteousness'. **Logizomai** is used 19 times in Romans, and 21 times elsewhere in the rest of the NT. It sometimes means 'think', 'consider' or 'reckon', and sometimes has a narrower sense, namely, 'set down to someone's account', hence 'put down', 'impute' or 'ascribe'. The ambiguity of 'to whom God reckons righteousness' is one of the reasons for the fierce battles between those who argue that justification is *making* someone righteous, and those who insist that it is merely *treating as* righteous.

'Independently of works', i.e. through faith.

[7, 8] The quotation is from Ps. 32.1, 2 (Sept. 31) with only one variation from the Septuagint, namely **hou**, 'of whom', instead of **hôi**, 'to whom'. Hence the second part of v. 8, literally translated, is 'whose [sin] the Lord will not put down as sin'. **Hou** is found in some of the best manuscripts, although several have **hôi**.

[9] 'Over', **epi**, or 'on', AV 'upon', because one makes a blessing over the person whom one is pronouncing happy.

'Circumcised' and 'uncircumcised', literally, 'circumcision' and 'uncircumcision'.

[10] The significance of Abraham being justified while he was still uncircumcised and, indeed, at a time before Moses received the tablets of the Law on Sinai is that it proves that a person can be justified, firstly, while he is outside the Mosaic Law, because it had not yet come into existence, and secondly, without being circumcised.

11 And he received the sign of circumcision as the seal of justification by faith while in an uncircumcised state, so that he might be the father of all those who believe while in an uncircumcised state, [and] so that they might be accounted righteous, 12 and the father also of the circumcised, those who are not only circumcised but who walk in the steps of the faith of

our father the uncircumcised Abraham. 13 For the promise that he should inherit the world [was] not [given] to Abraham or his seed through the Law but through justification by faith. 14 For if those relying on the Law inherit, faith is made ineffective and the promise has been cancelled.

[11] The metaphors of 'sign', **sêmeion**, and 'seal', **sphrâgîda**, are not as straightforward as they might appear. At first sight one might take **sêmeion** as the impression left by the seal, **sphrâgîs**, but Paul actually refers to the sign as though it were the seal itself. The explanation is simple: the word **sphrâgîs** can denote either the instrument that makes the impression, e.g. a signet ring, or the impression left in the wax attached to the document. In Revelation, where the word is used thirteen times, it seems for the most part to denote the latter. Paul uses it in I Cor. 9.2 to describe his audience as the seal of his apostleship, presumably as the impression left on a document which certifies that he is an apostle. Abraham's circumcision then was the mark made by the wax impression or stamp on the certificate defining his justification by faith. The notion that circumcision was the sign of the new and everlasting covenant which God had made with Abraham comes from Gen. 17.11, and the same word **sêmeion** is used in the Sept. version of that verse.

'Justification by faith', **tês dikaiosynês tês pisteos**, literally, 'the righteousness of faith'. The phrase also occurs in v. 13, but without the definite articles.

'So that they might be accounted righteous', **eis to logisthê-nai autois dikaiosynên**, literally, 'for the purpose of putting down to them righteousness'. Some manuscripts add **kai**, 'also', before **autois**, as we can see in the AV and the Vulgate, but it is probably best to leave it out as most good manuscripts do. I have kept the awkward repetition of 'so that' in this verse to indicate that Paul uses the **eis to** construction with the infinitive twice.

[12] This verse refers to Jewish Christians, who have obviously been circumcised, but who exhibit the faith shown by Abraham at a time when he was still uncircumcised. Jerome, however, takes 'circumcised' figuratively, and adds 'in the heart', applying the description to all Gentile believers.

'Of the faith of our father the uncircumcised Abraham', literally, 'of the faith in uncircumcision of our father Abraham'. Jerome observes, 'He was righteous while an uncircumcised man, so that he should be father of the uncircumcised, and remained righteous when circumcised, so that he might become father of the righteous circumcised.'

[13] 'The promise', **epangeliâ**, as I point out in my notes on Gal. 3.14, is an appropriate word to use here because it denotes a free offer from one party, not a pledge which has been agreed on by two parties. The word is often found in the plural when referring to the promises of Abraham, because God made more than one promise, e.g. that he would found a great nation in a new land (Gen. 12.1–7), and that he would be the father of many nations (Gen. 17.4–6). The meaning of the statement 'the promise was not given through the Law' is that Abraham was not circumcised at the time when he received the promise, and therefore, as circumcision was a commandment of the Law, the Law was not in force and could not have been the vehicle through which the promise operated.

'That he should inherit the world', **klêronomon auton einai kosmou**, is most probably derived from Gen. 12.1–7, where God tells Abraham that he should go to 'the land that I will show you', and from Gen. 15.7, where God tells him that he brought him out of the land of the Chaldaeans 'to give you this land *to inherit* (**klêronomêsai**)'. 'This land' was interpreted as representing the world to come. The rabbis taught that Abraham had taken possession of this *and the future world* as a reward of faith, as Käsemann points out. Hebrews 11.8–10 is particularly relevant because it says that when Abraham was 'called to go out to a place which he was to receive as his inheritance', he went out and settled 'as a foreigner in the land of promise as in a strange land', because he 'awaited the city with foundations, whose architect and creator was God'.

[14] 'Those relying on the Law', literally, 'those from the Law', **hoi ek nomou**.

'Is made ineffective', **kekenôtai**, literally, 'has been emptied', AV 'is made void'. In other words, if one could gain this inheritance by observing the Law, faith would be redundant.

'Has been cancelled', **katêrgêtai**; see note on 3.3 regarding this verb. If faith were redundant, the promise which came about because of faith would also be redundant.

15 For the Law earns retribution; but where there is no Law, [there is] no transgression [of it] either. 16 That is why [it comes] from faith, in order that [it may be] according to grace, so that the promise may be secured for all his seed, not for those who are only of the Law, but for the ones who are also of the faith of Abraham, who is the father of all of us, 17 as it is written, 'I have appointed you the father of many nations', [and this] in the presence of the God in whom he had faith, who brings the dead to life, and who calls things which do not exist into existence.

[15] It might be helpful to flesh out this point in more detail: the only thing which the Law can do is to define sin, and as everyone breaks the Law, everyone faces punishment; but if

the Law is superseded, one cannot break it, and so there can be no punishment for breaking it.

'Earns retribution', **orgên katergazetai**, literally, 'effects anger'; see note on 1.18.

[16] Note the absence both of a subject and of verbs in the original. What [comes] from faith? The inheritance, as Jerome suggests? Justification? Probably both.

'That is why', **dia touto**, i.e. 'because of this', refers to the previous statement that the Law can only earn retribution.

'So that the promise may be' could also be 'with the result that the promise is'. This is the same **eis to** construction we met in v. 11.

'Secured', **bebaiân**, literally, 'firm', 'secure'.

'Those' and 'the ones' are singular in the original because they refer to the singular 'seed', **spermati**, i.e. his descendants.

[17] The quotation is from Gen. 17.5.

Some commentators think that the phrase '*in the presence of* (**katenanti**) (the) God' refers to some part of the previous verse. Lightfoot, for example, believes that it qualifies the clause 'so that the promise may be secured for all his seed'. Similarly, the NEB has 'this promise, then, was valid before God'. There is, however, no real problem here. It is only when he is referring to God's presence, e.g. II Cor. 12.19, 'we are speaking *before* God', that Paul uses the word **katenanti**, which usually has the meaning 'over against', 'opposite'. Here it must refer to the fact that Abraham was in the actual presence of God when God told him that he would be the father of many nations. We are told in Gen. 17.1 that God actually *was seen* by Abraham, hence God's prophecy has extra significance for Paul.

'Brings the dead to life' is full of meaning. In the first place, Abraham's faith is linked to faith in the resurrection, and especially the resurrection of Christ. Secondly, it anticipates the statement in v. 19 that Abraham did not let the fact that his own body was virtually dead, nor the deadness of Sarah's womb, stand in the way of his faith. Thirdly, it reminds us of the rabbinic tradition that, when Abraham offered his son Isaac in sacrifice, Isaac actually died and was brought to life when God said 'Lay not thine hand upon the lad,' Gen. 22.12 (AV). Heb. 11.19 says of Abraham, 'He reckoned that God was able to raise him (Isaac) even from the dead, from which, figuratively, he did recover him.'

'Who calls things which do not exist into existence', **kalountos ta mê onta hôs onta**, literally, 'calling the things which are not as being'. I do not hesitate to add 'into' after 'calls', since 'calls' here means 'calls forth', as we can see from the many versions of this clause which Käsemann cites from Jewish literature. For instance, Philo (*On the Special Laws*, 4.187) says, 'For he called that which was not into being', **ta gar mê onta ekalesen eis to einai.** The early church adopted this formula and we find in a letter wrongly attributed to Clement of Rome, II Clem. 1.8, 'For *he called* (**ekalesen**) us *while we did not exist* (**ouk ontas**) and willed us to exist *from that which does not exist* (**ek mê ontos**).' We also read in The Shepherd of Hermas (*Vision* I, 1.6) that God created 'from that which is not, that which is', **ek tou mê ontos ta onta.** See also my notes on Heb. 11.3 in *Reading through Hebrews*. What are the things which God creates from nothing in this passage? Abraham's son Isaac, as Jerome points out, and, of course, his descendants. There is also another point which Paul is making: the dogma 'God created what is from what is not' deliberately contradicts the common maxim, current in Greek philosophy, that 'nothing comes from what is not; but everything is from what is'. In other words, Jews and Christians alike saw that to believe that something has always existed from which other things can arise was a denial of God's creative power.

18 Against hope [yet] in hope he believed, so that he became the father of many nations according to the saying, 'so will be your seed', 19 and, without weakening in faith, although he perceived his own body which was already virtually dead, since he was about a hundred years old, and the deadness of Sarah's womb, 20 he did not waver in disbelief regarding the promise of God, but was empowered by faith, giving God the glory. 21 He was completely assured that what God had promised he also could do. 22 That is why it was indeed 'put down to him as righteousness'. 23 'It was put down to him' was not only written on his account, 24 but also for us, to whom it is to be 'put down', believing, as we do, in him who raised from the dead our Lord Jesus, 25 who was surrendered for our sins and raised for our justification.

[18] 'Against hope', **par'elpida**, and 'in hope', **ep'elpidi**, are meant to contrast with each other. 'In hope' is not the object of the verb 'he believed'.

'The saying' is from Gen. 15.5 and comes immediately after the part where God tells Abraham to look up to heaven and count the stars, 'if you can'. There is also another significance in the shortened quotation: 'so will be your seed' can mean that Abraham's descendants will share in the promises along with him. If his faith is put down as righteousness, his descendants also will be justified through faith.

[19] 'Perceived', **katenoêsen**, NEB 'contemplated'. The AV 'he considered not', in modern idiom 'disregarded', is based on a text which included the word 'not', **ou**.

'Virtually dead', **nenekrômenon**, literally, 'dead', 'morti-
fied', is used also to describe Abraham in Heb. 11.12.

'About a hundred years old'; actually he was ninety-nine
when he received the promise of his second son Isaac.

Sarah is very important in Jewish tradition, as I mention in
my notes in *Reading through Galatians* on the elaborate
allegory Paul outlines in Gal. 4.22–26. Hebrews 11.11 states
that Sarah also had faith that she would bear a child.

[20] 'Was empowered by faith', **enedynamôthê têi pistei**, is
preferable to the NEB and AV 'strong in faith'. Most people
would take 'strong in faith' as referring to the strength of his
faith, not to the fact that he was given the power to achieve a
miracle by his faith.

'Giving God the glory' is not just 'glorifying God'; it means
attributing all the credit for the miracle to God. Of course,
Abraham was given the power to achieve the miracle, but the
power was given to him by God. This is precisely the point
Paul is making in Col. 1.29, 'To this end I toil and strive
according to his working that works in me with power.' Paul's
efforts are the manifestation of the powers given to him by
God.

[21] 'He was completely assured', **plêrophorêtheis**, literally,
'having been fulfilled', is a secondary meaning of this verb.
This is the sense it also carries in 14.5 and in I Clem. 42.3,
'fully assured through the resurrection', **plêrophorêthentes dia
tês anastaseôs**. See my notes on Col. 2.2 and 4.12 regarding
this verb and its cognate noun **plêrophoriâ** in *Reading through
Colossians and Ephesians*.

[22–24] The text which underpins this chapter is now applied
to us; Abraham is not the only one for whom it is relevant.
This prepares the ground for the next theme, namely, how
justification by faith affects us. The faith (**pistis**) through

which our justification has been effected is manifested in the
fact that we believe (**tois pisteuousin**) that God raised Jesus
from the dead. The AV 'if we believe' stresses the condition on
which justification is offered. Paul, however, is not holding
out the possibility of our belief, but assuming that we already
do believe.

[25] 'Was surrendered', **paredothê,** or 'was betrayed'. The
NEB (1961) has 'he was delivered to death', which in the
1970 edition was altered to 'he was given up'. In Eph. 5.2 and
5.25 Paul says that Christ 'gave himself', **paredôken heauton,**
but this is in the context of offering himself for sacrifice. There
seem to be two ideas running together here: firstly, the idea of
a sacrificial offering, and secondly, the betrayal of Christ to
his enemies. The latter is clearly the sense intended in I Cor.
11.23, 'on the night when *he was betrayed* (**paredideto**)'. Paul
most probably is recalling the words of Isa. 53.12 (Sept.), 'his
soul *was handed over* (**paredothê**) to death, and he was
numbered among the transgressors, and himself bore the sins
of many, and *because of* (**dia**) their sins *was he handed over*
(**paredothê**)'. In this case, the idea of betrayal and the idea of
sacrifice are inextricably linked together.

'For our sins', **dia ta paraptômata hêmôn,** i.e. *'because of'*,
not 'on behalf of'.

'For our justification', i.e. 'so that we might be justified'.
This is one of only two cases where **dikaiôsis,** the technical
term for 'justification', is used in the NT, as I point out in the
notes to 1.17. Elsewhere Paul uses the word **dikaiosynê,**
'righteousness', to denote 'justification'.

Chapter 5

1 So, being justified by faith, we are at peace with God through our Lord Jesus Christ, 2 through whom indeed we have been introduced by faith into this grace in which we stand, exulting in our hope of the glory of God; 3 not only that, but even exulting in our afflictions, knowing as we do that affliction produces endurance, 4 and endurance proof, and proof hope. 5 [Our] hope does not shame [us], because the love of God has been poured out in our hearts through the Holy Spirit which has been given to us.

[1] 'We are at peace', **eirênên echomen**, literally, 'we have peace'. There is no longer a state of enmity between us and God; we are no longer on opposite sides. The text, unfortunately, presents us with another problem: there is strong manuscript evidence for the reading **echômen**, '*let us* have' (subjunctive), hence the NEB 'let us continue at peace', and it appears that both Chrysostom and Jerome had a subjunctive in their texts. Robinson claims that the manuscript evidence is 'overwhelmingly in favour' of the subjunctive, but this is an exaggeration. In fact, there are good manuscripts with the indicative **echomen**. I believe that Paul is describing the new state of affairs, namely, that we are no longer enemies of God, since we have been reconciled to him by Christ. The

subjunctive would imply that it is action on our part that enables us to make peace with God.

[2] 'We have been introduced', **tên prosagôgên eschêkamen**, literally, 'we have had the introduction'. **Prosagôgê** is not just 'access'; it denotes the act of an official introducing someone into the presence of a ruler. See my note on Eph. 2.18 in *Reading through Colossians and Ephesians*.

'Exulting', **kai kauchômetha**, literally, 'and we boast'. Some believe that 'grace' is the object in which we exult, but the word order suggests that we take this verb with 'hope'. 'Boasting of' would be quite an acceptable alternative for 'exulting in', since Paul frequently uses this verb **kauchaomai**, which is usually translated as 'I boast', in a good sense, e.g. Gal. 6.14, 'Far be it from me to boast except of the cross of our Lord Jesus Christ.' Some translators take **kauchômetha** as a subjunctive, i.e. 'let us exult', since the indicative and subjunctive of this class of Greek verb in the present tense are identical, but Jerome has *gloriamur*, which has to be indicative in Latin.

'The glory of God' is the glory which we hope God will give us.

[3] 'Exulting', **kauchômetha** again. The same question occurs as the one in the previous verse – is it indicative or subjunctive?

'Endurance', **hypomenên**, which could also be 'patience' or 'fortitude'.

[4] 'Proof', **dokimên**, a difficult word to translate. Barclay translates it as 'character' and the AV as 'experience', but neither is quite right, although Barclay is closer. The Vulg. *probationem*, 'approval' or 'appraisal', is closer still. Paul uses this word four times in II Corinthians and once in Philippians. It is not found anywhere else in the NT, but the

verb **dokimazô** is found twenty-two times with such meanings as 'test', 'prove for oneself', 'scrutinize', 'examine' or
'approve'. So the noun should mean 'proof' or 'approved
character' (which is not the same as 'character' plain and
simple), and here refers to the fact that by enduring suffering
one emerges like gold from the furnace, tested and guaran-
teed as genuine. Looking at it from the point of view of the
person who has been through this trial, one has tested one's
faith and proved it to be real; from the point of view of
God, the person who has endured has passed the test
successfully.

[5] The notion of 'shame' may seem odd, but Paul is making
the point that our hope of final glory is not something of
which we are ashamed. He is probably alluding to Ps. 25. 20
(Sept. 24), 'Guard my soul and deliver me; *let me not be put to
shame*, because *I have put my hope* in you', or Ps. 22.5 (Sept.
21.6), 'They cried out to you, and were saved; *they hoped in
you and were not put to shame.*' Others may ridicule us for
hoping to be resurrected in glory, for pinning our hopes on
Christ, but we disregard them. In this reference to shame,
there is also the idea of not being ashamed on the Day of
Judgment, i.e. of being vindicated.

'Love of God' could be either 'love for God' or 'God's love
for us'. Commentators, such as Sanday and Headlam, tend to
argue for one or the other, but this is a false dichotomy. This
love starts as God's love towards us, but becomes, when we
respond, the love we have for him and for others. This love is
not a mere feeling, but a way of life which is characterized by
acts of love, and one which does not put us to shame since
even our enemies admire it.

6 For, at a time when we were still powerless, even
then did Christ die for [us] sinners. 7 For one will

scarcely go to one's death for a righteous person, although perhaps one might even be brave enough to do so for a good one. 8 But God demonstrates his love towards us, in that, while we were still sinners, Christ died for us. 9 So, having been justified now by his blood, we shall much more certainly be saved through him from the wrath [to come]. 10 For if we were reconciled to God through the death of his son, while we were enemies, much more certainly shall we, being reconciled, be saved by his life, 11 and not only that, but also [saved] as we exult in God through our Lord Jesus Christ, through whom we have now received our reconciliation.

[6] 'At a time when . . . even then', **eti . . . eti kata kairon**, literally, 'still . . . still at the time', is an unusual idiom, and the large number of variations in the text indicate that it was hard to understand from the beginning. One of the difficulties is the fact that the phrase **kata kairon** commonly meant 'in season', i.e. 'at the right time', hence the AV 'in due time' and Lightfoot's 'at the proper time'. The Vulg. *secundum tempus*, 'according to the time' could support either interpretation. We do, however, have evidence from inscriptions that the phrase also meant simply 'at the time' or 'then', and the NEB and Käsemann take it in this sense.

'Powerless', **asthenôn**, because we had not yet received the power of the Holy Spirit, and also because we were incapable of doing anything to put ourselves right with God. The word can also mean 'weak', 'feeble' or 'ill'. In Heb. 7.28 the 'weakness', **astheneia**, of the high priests established by the Mosaic Law is contrasted with the powerful ministry of Christ.

'Sinners', **asebôn**; see note on 4.5.

[7] The contrast between 'righteous', **dikaiou**, and 'good', **agathou**, in this verse is at first sight hard to follow. Why would one be more willing to sacrifice one's life for a 'good' person than a 'righteous' one? Presumably because goodness is more than righteousness: a good man is not merely a decent law-abiding person; he goes out of his way to do good to others. Hence the good man is more popular and so one might be more willing to sacrifice one's life for him. The argument, however, is irrelevant, since the important point is that, while we might be prepared to die for a good or righteous person, Christ actually died for sinners. Some commentators such as Barrett have suggested that the first part of this verse was written down from dictation and should have been deleted when Paul corrected himself and dictated the second part to replace it. Unfortunately, this ingenious suggestion is totally unsupported by any evidence.

[8] 'Demonstrates', **synistêsin**; see note on 3.5.
    'Sinners' this time is **hamartôlôn**.

[9] This verse clearly distinguishes between the initial justification or redemption of sinners, which has been brought about by Christ's death, and their final redemption. The former is referred to in 3.24, 'and are justified freely by his grace through the redemption by Christ Jesus', and the latter in 8.23, 'we, too, groan inwardly as we await our adoption, the redemption of our bodies'.

[10] The contrast here is between the death and life of Christ. His death brought about our reconciliation with God, when we ceased to be enemies; the life is the life which Christ lives in his church, the life into which we rose when we died to sin in baptism. This life is eternal life and is the life by which we are raised at our final resurrection.
    'We were reconciled', **katêllagêmen**, from the verb **katal-**

lassô, 'I change', which was commonly used in Greek literature to denote the change from enmity to friendship. So 'to reconcile' is 'to change an enemy into a friend'. It is only found in the NT in Paul's letters, here in Romans, once in I Corinthians and three times in II Corinthians (the variant **apokatallassô** is found in Colossians and Ephesians). The noun **katallagê**, 'reconciliation', found in the next verse, is also only used by Paul in the NT.

[11] Most translations slide over the difficulty presented by the missing main verb in this verse and treat **kauchômenoi**, 'as we exult', i.e. 'exulting', as though it meant 'we exult'. In some manuscripts it was even altered into **kauchômetha**, 'we exult', in order to act as a main verb. The most likely solution, however, is to assume that the verb 'we shall be saved' of the previous verse is to be understood as repeated in this verse.

The point Paul seems to be making is that our response when we are finally saved need not be that of cringing suppliants begging for mercy, since we have already been reconciled, but that of faithful servants who are triumphantly proud to have such a God as Lord. Jerome speaks of our receiving not only eternal life but also the promise of a sort of 'divine glory', *quaedam similitudo divinae gloriae*.

12 As a result, just as sin came into the world through one human being, and death [came in] through sin, so also did death spread over all mankind, as a consequence of the fact that everyone sinned. 13 For sin was in the world until the time of the Law, but it is not counted as sin if there is no Law. 14 Yet death ruled from Adam until Moses, even over those who had not committed a transgression like that of Adam, who is the type of the one who was to come. 15 But the

favour bestowed is not like the sin; for if the many
died through one person's sin, much more abundant
was the grace of God and the free gift [bestowed] on
the many by the grace of the one man Jesus Christ.

[12] 'As a result', **dia touto**, literally, 'because of this', leads
us to expect a statement which links the preceding argument
with one relating to the gift of life which Christ has given, and
so after the introduction of a comparison 'just as sin (and
death) came into the world because of one human being', we
would expect a conclusion such as 'so did righteousness (and
life) come into the world by one man'. Paul, however, as he so
often does, interrupts himself to develop the connection
between death and sin. He returns to the uncompleted
comparison in v. 15.

'As a consequence of the fact that everyone sinned', **eph'hôi
pantes hêmarton**, is not difficult to understand. One human
being, Adam, sinned and the result was that he (eventually)
died; everyone since Adam has also sinned, and so has died.
Paul does not say that death spread throughout mankind just
because they were descendants of Adam, but because they
also were sinners. Nor does he say that all men sinned in
Adam, since it is impossible to take this clause as meaning '*in
whom* everyone sinned'. The Vulg. *eo quod omnes peccaver-
unt* also rules out such an interpretation. Jerome, incidentally,
regards Eve, not Adam, as the human being through whom sin
entered the world. Adam merely followed her example. God,
however, did not accept that as an excuse (Gen. 3.12–19).

[13] This verse answers the hypothetical question, 'But was
there sin in the world before the Mosaic Law existed?' Sin
existed, even though the Law defining sin had not yet
appeared.

'It is not counted', **ouk ellogeitai**, i.e. 'it is not entered into the account book', Vulg. *non imputatur*. This is the only place where the verb **ellogeô** occurs in the NT. There was a similar verb **ellogaô**, which occurs in Philemon 18, and the two are often confused; hence we find various readings in the manuscripts. It is odd that the tense is present, as we would have expected Paul to continue with 'was not counted', **ouk enelogeito**, and some manuscripts have that reading. The great majority of good manuscripts, however, have the present tense **ellogeitai**. Inconsistencies like this are common in Paul's letters, because he is often eager to make a new point. Here he probably means to complete the statement with the past tense, but breaks off to make the general observation that an infringement of a law cannot be recorded if that law has not yet come into force.

[14] 'Even over those who had not committed a transgression like that of Adam', in other words, 'even though their particular sin was not the same as Adam's sin'. Adam's particular sin was disobedience of a clear commandment from God.

'The type of the one who was to come', **typos tou mellontos**, is difficult. Leaving aside the implausible suggestion that **tou mellontos** means '*that which* was to come', there are two possible interpretations: the first is that the 'one who was to come' refers to Adam's descendants, and thus Adam, as a sinner is the prototype of all sinners. The second is that 'the one who was to come' is Christ. Following the first interpretation, as Adam is a 'type' of sinner, the 'one who was to come' must also be a sinner. Robinson has a variant of this: for him 'the one who was to come' is 'man under the law' or 'Mosaic man'. **Typos**, however, is ambiguous since, besides meaning 'sketch', 'outline', 'rough draft', and 'pattern', it tends to be used by Paul to mean 'example', sometimes an example *not* to be followed, as in I Cor. 10.6, and sometimes a good example to be imitated, as in Phil. 3.17 and I Thess. 1.7.

But if we say that Adam was an example of sin followed by those who were to come, surely Paul would have used the plural **tôn mellontôn**, 'the ones who were to come after him'?

When we consider the second interpretation, our first question must be 'how is Adam a **typos** of Christ?' Clearly it must be because Adam through his disobedience brought death into the world, and *by contrast*, Christ's obedience brought life. In other words, the correspondence between them is by *opposites*, not *similarities*. This is precisely the point made by Chrysostom, who defines the analogy by contrasting the introduction of death by the one with the provision of righteousness by the other. Jerome, however, in his search for an analogy by similarities, unconvincingly sees one in the fact that, just as Adam was created without any sexual act on the part of parents, so Christ was born of a virgin. He admits, however, that some commentators interpret the correspondence between Adam and Christ as being by opposites, giving as an example *sicut ille peccati caput, ita et iste iustitiae*, 'just as the one was the source of sin, so the other was [the source] of righteousness'. Whether the analogy is by opposites or similarities, the conclusion seems to be that the old man, Adam, foreshadows in some way the new man, Christ.

But it is not quite as simple as that: as I point out in my notes on Col. 3.10 and Eph. 4.13 in *Reading through Colossians and Ephesians*, in one of those passages the new man seems to be not Christ himself, but the human being who is patterned on Christ. Paul, however, is not consistent and seems to veer between the two ideas. In Eph. 4.13 'the perfect man' is probably Christ. Who, then, is 'the one who is to come' here? In I Cor. 15.22, 'as in Adam all die, so also in Christ all shall be made alive', and in I Cor. 15.45, 'the first man Adam was made a living soul, the last Adam a life-giving spirit', it is clear that Christ is 'the one who was to come'. The fact that in this passage of Romans Paul proceeds to contrast

Adam and Christ for the rest of the chapter makes this interpretation even more likely.

[15] 'Favour bestowed', **charisma**, AV 'free gift', NEB 'act of grace', Vulg. *donum*. In 1.11 I translate **charisma** as 'blessing'; as I point out in the note to that verse, it is, like **charis**, a word rich in meaning. The thinking behind this verse is very condensed. Paul is making the point that God's generous response in dealing with the sin of Adam is more than adequate for dealing with the consequences of his disobedience. Many have died since Adam sinned and brought death into the world, but many more will be saved by Christ.

16 And the gift is not like [the one resulting] through the individual who had sinned; for the judgment resulting from that one was for condemnation, while the favour resulting from many sins was for justification. 17 For if by one man's sin death ruled through that one, much more shall those who receive the abundance of grace and of the free gift of justification rule in life through the one Jesus Christ. 18 So, then, as through one sin condemnation [resulted] for all mankind, so also through one act of justice justification and life [resulted] for all mankind.

[16] Paul continues to develop elaborate analogies and antitheses. To put it crudely, in the previous verse the contrast is one of quantity: the grace of God is so abundant and generous that it exceeds the effects of the sin which it is designed to remedy. Here there are two contrasts: firstly, one of quality, i.e. the result of God's response is justification or acquittal, whereas the result of the original sin was condemnation; and secondly, one of quantity, the sins of the one contrasted with the sins of the many. Note that 'judgment',

krima, balances 'favour', **charisma**, and 'condemnation', **katakrima**, balances 'justification', **dikaiôma**. Note also that the 'gift' of God is contrasted with the (unstated) 'gift' of Adam. We may find the complexity and artificiality of this rhetorical style unattractive, but it was familiar to an ancient audience.

[17] This time Paul contrasts death with life, and Adam with Christ. He also contrasts death's reign ('ruled', **ebasileusen**) with the rule of those who have been saved ('shall rule', **basileusousin**).

'Justification' is, of course, also 'righteousness'.

[18] 'So, then', **ara oun,** ought to mark the conclusion of the preceding argument, but Paul continues with his contrasts and analogies to the end of the chapter. In this verse, however, he attempts to summarize briefly his main points so far: one man sinned, and all mankind was condemned; one man performed an act of justice, and all mankind was acquitted. The balance is not perfect due to the omission of 'death', the antithesis of 'life'.

'Through one sin' and 'through one act of justice' could also be 'through one man's sin' and 'through one man's act of justice' . Both the AV and the Vulgate favour the expanded version.

'Act of justice', **dikaiômatos**, is normally taken in this passage to mean 'justification', which is how I translate it in v. 16. In 1.32 it means 'judgment' and in 2.26 'decree'. The problem is that it can also mean 'penalty', i.e. a judgment against one. Is it possible that in this verse Paul is referring to the condemnation of Jesus by Pilate, an act which led to his death? Barclay paraphrases the word **dikaiômatos** as 'one supreme act of righteousness', and the Vulgate translates it as *iustitiam*, which the AV's 'righteousness' clearly echoes.

'Justification and life', literally, 'justification of life'.

19 For, just as the many were made sinners by the disobedience of one man, so also by one man's obedience the many will be made righteous. 20 The Law came in so that the transgression might be in excess; and where sin was in excess, grace was super-abundant, 21 in order that, as sin reigned in death, so grace also might rule through justification for eternal life through our Lord Jesus Christ.

[19] The 'disobedience', **parakoês**, of Adam is contrasted with the 'obedience', **hypakoês**, of Christ. See the note on 1.5 regarding **hypakoê**.

'Were made', **katestathêsan**, or 'were presented as'.

[20] 'Came in', **pareisêlthen**, Vulg. *subintravit*, literally, 'came in beside'. The NEB 'intruded into this process' implies that the Law pushed its way in where it was not supposed to be, but the more likely sense is that it was 'by the way', as Lightfoot says, 'a temporary application, a partial dominion'. The verb **pareiserchomai** is used in medicine to describe the insertion of an instrument or fingers into the body.

'Transgression' is a specific act which breaks a law. Once the Law had defined a crime, instances of that crime were automatically totted up. The Law, however, merely highlighted or revealed sin which had existed from the time of Adam; it did not create sin.

'Was super-abundant', **hypereperisseusen**. As I point out in my note on Gal. 3.19 in *Reading through Galatians*, for Paul the primary function of the Law is providing knowledge of sin and so enabling grace to operate. As Chrysostom says, 'It was not that the punishment might be the greater, but that the grace might be seen to be the greater.'

[21] This verse summarizes his argument with a final antith-

esis: sin is answered by grace, and death by eternal life, a process of justification made possible by Christ. It is interesting that the next chapter also ends with a reference to eternal life and Jesus Christ.

Chapter 6

1 So what shall we say? Are we to continue in sin, so that there may be all the more grace? 2 God forbid! How shall we, who died to sin, go on living in it? 3 Do you not know that we, who have been baptized into Christ Jesus, have been baptized into his death? 4 We were, therefore, buried with him through baptism into death, so that, just as Christ was raised from the dead through the glory of his father, we too might walk in newness of life. 5 For, if we have become linked with [him] in a death like his, then we shall certainly be [partakers] of his resurrection, 6 knowing that our old self was crucified with [him], so that our body of sin might be abolished and that we might no longer serve sin.

[1] 'Are we to continue', **epimenômen** (subjunctive), is a better reading than the future **epimenoumen** which is represented by AV 'shall we continue', NEB 'shall we persist' and Vulg. *permanebimus*.

[2] 'Go on living', **eti zêsomen**, literally, '[shall we] still live'.

[3] 'Into', **eis**, denoting incorporation. Compare Gal. 3.27,

'For all of you who have been baptized into Christ have put on Christ.'

[4] Being buried in baptism is a dual process: one dies with Christ and is raised again. As Chrysostom succinctly observes, 'for baptism is the cross'. Compare Col. 2.12, 'buried together with him in that baptism in which you were also raised together [with him] through your faith in the action of God who raised him from the dead'. Furthermore, there are two stages involved in being raised again: firstly, one now shares in the new life of those who are in Christ, and secondly, one will be resurrected into eternal life on the last day. The first is referred to in this verse, 'walk in newness of life', i.e. 'live a new kind of life', and the second in the next verse. Incidentally, the NEB 'and lay dead' is a peculiar paraphrase of 'into death', **eis thanaton**, since it implies that at baptism rebirth is postponed.

'Through the glory of his father' could mean 'through his glorious father', or 'in the glory his father gave him'.

[5] 'Linked with [him]' is only one way of translating **symphytoi**; it could also mean 'born with', 'kindred' or 'grown together with'. The AV 'planted together', suggested probably by Jerome's *complantati*, is an attractive metaphor, recalling I Cor. 15.36–44, where Paul speaks of 'sowing' a physical body which is raised as a spiritual body. There is a cognate verb **symphyteuô**, 'I plant together', which does not occur in the NT, and a related verb **symphyô**, 'I grow together', which is found in Luke 8.7.

'In a death like his', literally, 'by the likeness of his death'.

'Then . . . certainly', **alla kai**, literally, 'but also'.

[6] 'Our old self ', **ho palaios hêmôn anthrôpos**, literally, 'our old man', occurs in Eph. 4.22, 'that you should put off the old man of your former life, who perishes in the pursuit of his

deceitful desires', and Col. 3.9, 'since you have put off the old man along with his deeds'.

'Body of sin', i.e. 'sinful body', is not to be taken as implying that our physical body is sinful because it is matter and not spirit. After all, the Christian who has died to sin by baptism into Christ still inhabits his physical body, although his 'body of sin' has been abolished. This expression reminds one of the phrase 'body of flesh' in Col. 2.11, 'And it is in him that you were circumcised with a circumcision not done by hands, but in the stripping off of the body of flesh in Christ's circumcision.' 'Body' here is not the physical body but rather a synonym for the complex word 'flesh', a word Paul uses when describing the essential nature of human beings as opposed to the nature of God, and which is often contrasted with 'spirit'. See my notes on Gal. 5.17 in *Reading through Galatians*.

'Might be abolished', **katargêthêi**; see note on 3.3.

7 For anyone who has died is set free from sin. 8 If we have died with Christ, we believe that we shall also be alive with him, 9 knowing that Christ, raised from the dead, dies no more; death has no longer any power over him. 10 For the death which he died, he died once and for all to sin, and the life which he lives, he lives to God. 11 Consider yourselves also in the same way as dead to sin and living to God in Christ Jesus.

[7] Paul provides further proof for the statement in the previous verse that by being crucified with Christ we are no longer slaves to sin. This maxim is clearly based on the rabbinical saying, 'When a man is dead he is freed from fulfilling the Law.' The argument is that, if a man's natural death frees him from the obligations of the Law because he can no longer be held accountable, his symbolic death in

baptism also frees him from sin for the same reason. We have died and thus are no longer under the rule of sin, nor, for that matter, subject to the Law.

'Is set free', **dedikaiôtai**, literally, 'has been acquitted'. See notes on Gal. 2.16 regarding this verb in *Reading through Galatians*.

[8, 9] The reasoning is as follows: 'Christ has died and been raised from the dead, and he cannot die a second time. Therefore, if we die with Christ, i.e. share his death, we shall be raised and live with him.' Note the tense of the verb in 'we shall also be alive with him', **kai syzêsomen autôi**, which focusses on the final resurrection from the dead in the future rather than our present new life in Christ. This is probably why Paul omits to say 'and *we* cannot die a second time' or 'death has no longer any power over *us*'; we have yet to experience our physical death. See the note on v. 4.

[10] 'The death which he died', **ho apethanen**, literally, 'that which he died', and 'the life which he lives', **ho zêi**, can be compared with Gal. 2.20, 'the life which I live', **ho zô**.

'He died to sin' means, as Lightfoot points out, that Christ died to a sinful world and to a life in which he bore the consequences of sin. The stress in this verse is on 'once and for all', **ephapax**, which reinforces the statements in the previous verse, 'dies no more' and 'death has no longer any power over him'.

[11] After explaining the theological implications of Christ's death and resurrection regarding the problem of sin, Paul now starts to tell his audience what their personal response should be in practical terms. Incidentally, this is the first time in this letter that I have translated the phrase **en Christôi** as 'in Christ', since in 3.24, where it also occurs, I translate the preposition **en** as 'by'. Its use here may indicate that Paul is

now turning from the individual on his own to the person incorporated in the body of the church. The phrase 'in Christ' (together with the related phrase 'in the Lord') is a remarkably complex and subtle expression. 'In Christ' can mean, firstly, something like 'as a Christian', i.e. as someone incorporated in the body of Christ and part of him; secondly, 'by the power of Christ' or 'inspired by Christ'; thirdly, 'through Christ' or 'with Christ acting as the channel'; and lastly, 'in the view of Christ', 'as Christ sees it'.

12 Do not, therefore, let sin rule in your mortal bodies with the result that you obey its desires, 13 and do not present your members to sin as weapons of wickedness, but present yourselves to God as people who are alive after being dead and your members to God as weapons of righteousness. 14 For sin shall not have any power over you, since you are not under the Law, but under grace.

[12] 'Bodies' is actually singular in the original, but 'your', i.e. 'of you', is plural, and 'body' would imply that Paul is addressing one person.

'Desires', **epithûmiais**, are the 'desires of the flesh' referred to in Eph. 2.3, 'amongst whom we, too, all lived once in the desires of our flesh, doing whatever our flesh and our minds wanted'. Although **epithûmiâ** is a morally neutral word, as I point out in the note to 1.24, the desires of the 'old man' are by their nature perverted and deceitful; as Eph. 4.22 says, 'put off the old man of your former life, who perishes in the pursuit of his deceitful desires.' This negative aspect of 'desire' is explored in chapter 7.

[13] 'Members', **melê**, are any parts of the body, not just arms and legs.

'Weapons', **hopla**, which can also be 'implements'.

'As people who are alive after being dead', **hôsei ek nekrôn zôntas**, literally, 'as if from corpses living', has two levels of meaning: firstly, it describes those who have symbolically died in baptism and have been resurrected into a new life. Secondly, it describes a hypothetical situation, since the expression 'as if', **hôsei**, could imply that they have not actually come back from the dead, but are being asked to act as though they had literally done so. Each meaning is valid and there is no need to reject one in favour of the other.

[14] 'Shall not have any power over you' echoes v. 9, 'has no longer any power over him'. But note the subtle difference: our complete freedom from death's power is still in the future, while Christ is already triumphant over death. Our final release from death's domination will be secured, not by subjecting ourselves to the Mosaic Law, but by relying on God's grace.

15 What then? Are we to sin because we are not under the Law but under grace? God forbid! 16 Do you not know that, if you present yourselves to someone as obedient slaves, you are the slaves of the one whom you obey, either of sin leading to death, or of obedience leading to righteousness? 17 Thanks be to God that you were the slaves of sin, but obeyed from the heart the form of teaching to which you were delivered, 18 and, being set free from sin, were made servants of righteousness.

[15] Paul raises a hypothetical question similar to the one put in v. 1, 'Are we to continue in sin, so that there may be all the more grace?' The difference is that the previous question posed the possibility of *remaining in a state of sin*; this one

suggests that one who has already made the transition to the rule of grace is free to *resume sinning* because he is no longer subject to the Law.

'Are we to sin', **hamartêsômen** (subjunctive), again (see v. 1) is a better reading than the future **hamartêsomen**, AV 'shall we sin', Vulg. *peccabimus*. This time the NEB goes for the subjunctive.

[16] Many commentators have pointed out that the antitheses in this verse are not what one would expect. 'Sin' is balanced by 'obedience', not 'righteousness', which would have been the obvious opposite, and 'death' is balanced by 'righteousness', not 'life'. As a result Paul gives us an implied contrast between 'obeying sin' and 'obeying obedience', the latter of which sounds strange. Why did Paul avoid the obvious? Leaving aside the fact that his style is often idiosyncratic and tortuous, it must be because he wished to throw the emphasis on the word 'obedience', **hypakoê**, since he uses it twice in this verse together with the cognate verb 'you obey', **hypoakouete**. 'Obedience' is uppermost in his mind for at least three reasons: firstly, Adam's disobedience has been contrasted with Christ's obedience in the previous chapter; secondly, the metaphor of slaves which Paul develops in this section naturally suggests the idea of obedience; and thirdly, he is using the word almost as a synonym for 'faith', rather as he uses it in 1.5 and 15.18 to denote the response of believers when they have heard the gospel. If one substitutes 'faith' for 'obedience' in the last part of the verse, the antithesis becomes much clearer. See also my notes on 1.5.

'As obedient slaves', **doulous eis hypakoên**, literally, 'slaves for obedience'. Note that we can also translate **doulous** as 'servants'.

[17, 18] 'To which you were delivered', **eis hon paredothête**, NEB 'to which you were made subject', Vulg. *in quam traditi*

estis. The AV 'which was delivered you' is grammatically suspect. The verb **paradidômi** can mean 'I transmit', 'hand down' when referring to a body of doctrine, but here it is people who are being 'handed over'. The verb is appropriate in this context because it can be used to denote the handing over of slaves, either to magistrates for torture and interrogation, or to new masters. 'The form of teaching', therefore, may represent the new master. 'Being set free' from one master, i.e. 'sin', you have now been handed over to a new master, i.e. 'righteousness'. Note the deliberate paradox in the combination of 'being set free' and 'were made servants'. The expression 'whose service is perfect freedom' occurs to mind.

19 I am speaking in human terms because of the weakness of your flesh. For as you presented your members as slaves to impurity and to lawlessness for lawlessness, so you should present your members now as slaves to righteousness for sanctification. 20 For when you were slaves of sin, you were free in respect to righteousness. 21 So what did you gain then [from those things] of which you are now ashamed? For the end result of those things is death. 22 But now, being set free from sin, and being made servants of God, the fruit which you enjoy leads to sanctification and the end result is eternal life. 23 For the wages of sin are death, but the free gift of God is eternal life in Christ Jesus our Lord.

[19] 'I am speaking in human terms', **anthrôpinon legô**, is said by way of apologizing for using slavery as a metaphor for the relationship between the believer and God. Paul uses a similar expression in 3.5, **kata anthrôpon legô**, which is also found in Gal. 3.15, where he apologizes for a metaphor

derived from the law governing wills to illustrate the nature of the promise God gave to Abraham.

'Because of the weakness of your flesh', i.e. 'because you cannot understand such things unless they are expressed in parables or allegories', or, as Jerome says, 'because you are not yet able to hear anything fully divine'. Slavery is, of course, a poor analogy for the true relationship with God, but it is one that everybody can understand, and one that does express the gulf between a righteous and all-powerful God and sinful (and weak) human servants.

'Impurity', **akatharsiâi**, is usually immoral sexual activity. See the notes on 1.24 and on Gal. 5.19 in *Reading through Galatians*.

'To lawlessness for lawlessness', **têi anomiâi eis tên anom-iân**, in other words, 'to your master Wickedness for wicked purposes'. It would have made a neater antithesis without the phrase 'to lawlessness', but the repetition is deliberate. The NEB attempts to improve Paul's style by obscuring the repetition with 'lawlessness, *making for moral anarchy*'. Note also Paul's use of the word 'lawlessness' to denote wickedness. This is a reminder to those who accused Paul of antinomianism ('against-law-ism') that he did not advocate 'law-less-ness', despite the fact that he encouraged Christians to abandon the 'Law'.

[20] 'You were free in respect to righteousness', i.e. you may have been free from the rule of righteousness, but that was the only freedom you had.

[21] 'What did you gain', **tina karpon eichete**, literally, 'what fruit did you have'. Some commentators end the sentence there and treat the next part as the answer to the question, e.g. Käsemann, who divides this section, 'But what fruit did you have then? You must now be ashamed of it.'

'End result', **telos**, i.e. 'end' or 'goal'.

[22] The opening part of this verse repeats the paradox of v. 18.

[23] This verse summarizes and rounds off the argument of this chapter.

'Wages', **opsônia**, more accurately a soldier's food allowance partly paid in kind, suggests a military context. Similarly, 'free gift', **charisma**, is translated by Tertullian (*Against Marcion*, V, 8.5) *as donativum*, a word which is used to denote the special bonus given to soldiers on the emperor's birthday or other official celebrations. In his work *On the Resurrection* (47.7) he quotes this verse and describes death as the 'wages', *stipendia*, of sin, and eternal life as the 'free gift', *donativum*, of God. Whether this is a military metaphor or not, the meaning is clear: the servants of sin earn wages, but the servants of God receive grace, a free gift, something they have not earned and which they do not deserve.

Chapter 7

1 Don't you know, brothers and sisters, for I am speaking to people who know the Law, that the Law has power over a person while he or she is alive? 2 For a woman who is married to a husband is legally bound to him during his lifetime, but if he dies, she is freed from her husband's law. 3 So then, if she becomes another man's [wife] while her husband is still alive, she will be called an adulteress; but if her husband dies, she is freed from the law and is not an adulteress, although she belongs to another man.

[1] The reference to 'people who know the Law' is further evidence that the audience Paul is addressing is a largely Jewish one, despite Robinson's assertion that it is not necessary to assume that Paul must be referring here to people with a Jewish background. The Law here, as elsewhere, is the Mosaic Law, although Sanday and Headlam suggest that Paul is referring to 'a general principle of all Law; . . . that death clears all scores'. Of course, non-Jews also believed that legal obligations were cancelled by death, but Paul would hardly appeal to Gentile practice if he wished to persuade the Judaizers in his audience. Furthermore, the whole passage is about the cancellation of the obligations of the *Torah*. He is obviously recalling the earlier statement in 6.7 that anyone

who has died is free from sin, and the underlying rabbinic argument, 'When a man is dead he is freed from fulfilling the Law.' The effect of death on the marriage contract between husband and wife provides a specific illustration of the way in which the obligation to observe the Law is cancelled by the death in baptism of the believer in Christ. Commentators have made heavy weather of the analogy, but it is not difficult to follow, provided one does not expect all the details to fit perfectly.

[2] 'Her husband's law', or, as Barclay translates it, 'the law concerning her husband', is an abbreviation for the 'legal contract she has with her husband'.

[3] The main point here is that after the death of her first husband a widow is free to marry another husband. In other words, *his* death cancels *her* legal obligations. Strictly speaking, if Paul wishes to illustrate the principle that the law has power over a person while he or she is alive, it should be the dead man, not his wife, who is freed from the legal obligation, and if we identify the wife with the Jew who becomes a Christian, she would have to die herself in order to marry her new husband, Christ. But all this is pressing the analogy too far. Paul was not trying to produce a perfect allegory with exact parallels.

4 So you, too, my brothers and sisters, have been put to death in regard to the Law through the body of Christ and belong to another, the one who was raised from the dead, in order that we can bear fruit to God. 5 For when we were in the flesh, our sinful impulses, [which existed] due to the Law, used to act in our members to bear fruit to death; 6 but now, because we have died, we have been released from the Law, by

which we were held, and so we serve in a new spirit, not in some ancient code.

[4] 'You have been put to death', **ethanatôthête**, Vulg. *mortificati estis*, a verb used particularly to denote death by execution. The NEB 'you have died' misses the force of the original. Paul uses this verb three times in Romans and once in II Corinthians, and in each case it means 'put to death' or 'execute'. Notice also the shift from the second person 'you have been put to death' to the first person 'we can bear fruit'. This anomaly is typical of Paul's style.

'Through the body of Christ' is a far from simple phrase. The choice of the preposition 'through', **dia**, rather than 'in', **en**, seems to indicate a process rather than a state. The possible meanings are as follows:

1. through the body of the church, i.e. as the mystical body of Christ;
2. through the death of Christ, i.e. by Christ's body being crucified;
3. through Christ's incarnation, i.e. through Christ taking bodily form;
4. through dying with Christ, i.e. by sharing his death;
5. through the sacrament of Christ's body, i.e. by partaking of his body.

There is a similar phrase in Col. 1.22, 'he has now reconciled again *in the body* of his flesh through his death'. Note that the phrases 'through his death' in Colossians and 'you have been put to death' in this verse define the context. Compare also Eph. 2.16, 'and reconcile again the two to God *in one body* through the cross', where again 'through the cross' gives us the clue to the correct interpretation. So the most likely interpretation here is a combination of 1, 2 and 4: Christ has died and we, as the body of Christ, have died with him.

Chrysostom explains 'through the body' by quoting from II Cor. 5.14, 'one died for all'. This would appear to favour interpretation 2, but, as we know from other remarks by Chrysostom, e.g. his comment on 6.4 that 'baptism is the cross', this should not be taken as a rejection of the other interpretations. 'Both . . . and' is often a better criterion than 'either . . . or' when interpreting Paul's thought.

'Belong to another', **genesthai heterôi**, recalls 'becomes another man's [wife]', **genêtai andri heterôi**, and 'although she belongs to another man', **genomenên andri heterôi** in v. 3. Clearly the wife and the new husband of that verse are identified here respectively with the Christian/the church and Christ. For a more developed version of the metaphor of the church as the bride of Christ see Eph. 5.25–32 and my notes on that passage in *Reading through Colossians and Ephesians*.

[5] 'When we were in the flesh', i.e. before we died to the flesh, since we are now living in the spirit.

'Our sinful impulses', **ta pathêmata tôn hamartiôn**, literally 'the troubles of sins'. There is a close correspondence between **pathêmata** and 'desires', **epithûmiai**; regarding the latter see the note on 6.12. Compare also Gal. 5.24, 'Those who are of Christ have crucified the flesh together *with its troubles* (**tois pathêmasin**) and desires.' The connection between the Law and sinful impulses is explored later in this chapter.

[6] 'Because we have died'; see the notes on v. 1 regarding the cancellation of legal obligations when a death occurs. The NEB 'having died to that which held us bound, we are discharged from the law' implies that something other than the Law held us bound. 'Sin' or 'the flesh' are possible, but both of them are feminine and the relative pronoun 'by which' is masculine or neuter. Hence the masculine 'Law' is more likely and recalls the phrase 'having been put to death in regard to the Law' in v. 4.

'We have been released from', **katêrgêthêmen apo**, is an interesting verb. The root meaning of **katargeô** is 'I make unemployed', 'I make redundant', hence 'I nullify', 'I abolish'. With the preposition **apo** it means 'I separate from', 'I sever from' (see Gal. 5.4).

'In a new spirit', **en kainotêti pneumatos**, recalls 'in newness of life', **en kainotêti zôês**, of 6.4.

'Not in some ancient code', **ou palaiotêti grammatos**, literally, 'not oldness of letter', refers to the obsolete Mosaic code.

7 So what shall we say? 'The Law is sin'? Perish the thought. But I would not have recognized sin, if [it had] not [been] through the Law. For I would not have been acquainted with covetousness, if the Law did not say, 'You shall not covet'. 8 But sin, taking a hold through the commandment, produced in me every kind of covetousness; for without the Law sin is dead. 9 I once was alive without the Law, but when the commandment arrived, sin came alive 10 and I died, and the commandment that was meant for life, was found in me to be for death; 11 for sin, taking hold through the commandment, cheated me and killed me through it.

[7] Paul is careful to avoid identifying the Law with sin, because the Law was given to Moses by God. Its main function was to define sin, and to act as a 'minder' until such a time as Christ should come (see Gal. 3.22–25).

Note the subtle difference between 'I would not have recognized', **ouk egnôn**, and 'I would not have been acquainted with', **ouk êidein**. The latter implies 'I would not have had any personal acquaintance with it', the former, 'I would not have known that it existed'. Jerome states that Paul here is speaking in the *persona* of someone who has accepted the Law.

I have kept the archaic translation 'covetousness' for **epithûmiân**, because it is cognate with 'covet', which is the verb one associates with the tenth commandment; see also the notes on 6.12.

'You shall not covet', **ouk epithûmêseis**, from Ex. 20.17 and Deut. 5.21. The use of this particular commandment to represent all of the commandments is found elsewhere in Jewish writers. For instance, Philo, speaking of the commandment against covetousness (*On the Ten Commandments*, 142), says, 'all the passions of the soul are difficult to deal with, since they disturb and shake it out of its natural state and prevent it from being healthy, but covetousness (**epithû-miâ**) is the most difficult'.

[8] 'Hold', **aphormên**, literally, 'starting point' or 'base of operations', hence 'foothold'. Once the commandment 'you shall not covet' has been established, covetousness is possible, and because of human weakness, likely to occur. Before one is aware that covetousness is a sin, it does not exist, i.e. 'sin is dead'. Animals, or small children, cannot sin because they do not know what is sinful.

[9, 10] Is Paul referring to himself when he says 'I once was alive', or is it meant to be what anyone might say? 'I' in Paul's letters is usually autobiographical, and the reference to the Law fits a Jewish context, which is supported by Jerome's statement regarding v. 7, but it does not materially affect the argument if Paul intended this to be taken as something which all human beings can say. Some commentators believe that 'I' in this section stands for 'Adam', but such an interpretation hardly fits the details, particularly those relating to a commandment which Adam did not know.

'I was alive' is more accurate than 'I lived', because he is emphasizing the contrast between 'life' and 'death', i.e. 'when sin was dead, I was alive, but when sin came alive, I died'. Sin comes alive with the Law, i.e. 'the commandment', so Paul must mean that when he was a small child he was not aware of the Law, but once he learned what the Law commanded, and was aware of sin, sin became alive for him, with the result that he underwent a spiritual death, as Jerome says, 'when I grew up, and began to be under the Law'. There is no need to assume that this happened specifically at Paul's *bar mitzvah*, since awareness of sin surely occurs before the age when a Jewish boy officially undertakes the observance of the Law. Chrysostom defines this time as 'before Moses', i.e. before he knew the Mosaic Law.

'I died' obviously cannot be taken literally, as referring to physical death, but as describing the spiritual death of those who have not yet believed the gospel and been baptized. It is not necessary to visualize such persons as being conscious that they have died spiritually. Paul clearly is describing his spiritual state in the eyes of God, a state of which he was unaware, since he was still enthusiastically observing the *Torah* before his conversion.

'Meant for life', because God's purpose in giving the Law was to save his people.

[11] 'Cheated', **exêpatêsen**, is a compound of the verb Eve uses when she says to God in Gen. 3.13 (Sept.), 'The snake *deceived* (êpatêse) me, and I ate.' The same compound verb is used again to describe Eve's deception in II Cor. 11.3 and I Tim. 2.14. This deception occurs on several levels, as Barclay points out: firstly, sin falsely claims to offer satisfaction and happiness; secondly, it fools one into thinking a certain act is not really sinful; thirdly, it deceives one into thinking one can get away with it. I would add a fourth level of deception, and the one most likely here, namely, that it

conceals from the sinner the fact that it brings about his
spiritual death.

'Through it', i.e. operating through the commandment. If it
had not been defined as a sin, it would have had no
opportunity to be active.

12 So the Law is holy and the commandment holy,
righteous and good. 13 So did the good turn out to be
death for me? Never! But sin [did], in order that it
should be seen to be sin, causing my death through the
good, in order that sin might become superlatively
sinful through the commandment.

[12] Again Paul insists on the intrinsic goodness of the Law
and the individual commandment 'you shall not covet'. In this
insistence he is entirely consistent, since he never refers to the
Law as sinful. It was rendered obsolete when faith in Christ
superseded it, but that does not make it sinful. Chrysostom
says that the Law here is the Mosaic Law, not the natural law,
nor the commandment given in Paradise, as 'some say'.

[13] 'Causing my death through the good', i.e. by operating
through the framework provided by the good Law, sin
brought about my spiritual death.

'Superlatively', **kath'hyperbolên,** in other words, God had
determined that sin should be revealed for what it was by
allowing it a free hand, to go over the top, as it were.

14 For we know that the Law is spiritual, but I am
fleshly, sold to sin. 15 For I do not know what I am
doing, since I do not do what I want [to do] and do
what I hate [doing]. 16 But if I do what I do not want
[to do], I am admitting that the Law is good. 17 Now
it is no longer me acting but the sin living in me. 18

For I know that good does not live in me, that is, in my flesh, since I have the freedom to want [to do] good, but not [the freedom] to do it. 19 For I do not do the good which I want to do, but the evil which I do not want [to do]. 20 But if I do what I do not want [to do], it is no longer me acting but the sin which lives in me.

Several commentators have deduced from the fact that Paul now begins a passage which is entirely written in the present tense, that he is describing his present psychological state as a Christian convert. Augustine, and particularly Luther and his followers, interpreted the passage in this way. The early Greek commentators, however, took the view that Paul was describing the inner experience of the unregenerate or pre-Christian person. Chrysostom says of the words 'but I am fleshly' that Paul is 'giving us a sketch of a human being living his life in the Law (**en tôi nomôi**) and before the Law (**pro tou nomou**)'. Faced with such diverse interpretations, commentators have tended to be polarized on this issue. It would be beyond the scope of this guide to explore the controversy in great detail, but I should like to outline the main points which tend to be made:

1. There is a clear contrast between chapter 7, which lays out the gloomy problem, and chapter 8, which gives the joyful solution.
2. The use of the autobiographical 'I' continues; it is therefore reasonable to assume that Paul is still talking about himself, describing an actual or a hypothetical state of mind.
3. The use of the present tense may not indicate a real time shift; the present can be used to make a narrative more vivid without conveying any temporal significance.

4. If this is a description of Paul's mental state as a Christian it is totally different from all his other references to the life of a Christian, which is one that he always portrays as full of joy, peace, assurance and spiritual blessings, even though he also describes it frequently as fraught with danger, threatened with persecution and liable to trials and tribulations.
5. On the other hand, even committed Christians can know the internal struggle between good and evil. Why can this passage not describe such an experience?

Those interested in the arguments and counter-arguments of this controversy are recommended to read Robinson's discussion of this section. He concludes that the concentration on the time-reference, i.e. a past or a present experience, has put people on the wrong track. The real contrast, he thinks, is not between what I was and what I am, but between the Law and myself. The clue to understanding this passage is Paul's statement in this verse that 'the Law is spiritual (**pneumatikos**), but I am fleshly (**sarkinos**)'. In other words, the context here is the timeless battle between spirit and flesh, **pneuma** and **sarx**. It is therefore missing the main point to focus only on the question, 'Are these the thoughts of someone *before* or *after* conversion?' Paul is demonstrating that the person living in the flesh is incapable of free action, since only life in the spirit enables one to fulfil the spiritual Law. I would also suggest that Paul is still piling up evidence that the Law is good, in this instance by contrasting its goodness with the wickedness of sin. At the same time, and this is not a contradiction, he implies that the Law is powerless in the battle against sin.

In conclusion, I would like to put forward an interpretation which takes into account both sides in this controversy:

Those who take the view that Paul is describing the psychological experience of the unregenerate person are right, provided that they do not limit this to a particular time in that person's life, i.e. by confining it to a pre-Christian period. Those who believe that the passage describes Paul's present experience as a Christian are right, but only in so far as it is a hypothetical state, i.e. what he *would* feel, if he reverted to a 'fleshly' viewpoint. To put this another way, when Paul cries out in v. 24, 'What a pitiful creature I am! Who will save me from this body of death?', he is not describing his normal or his own emotions, but rather the reactions of someone who is trying to deal with the power of sin by relying on purely human resources. Some commentators regard the intensity of emotion in this outburst as an indication of heartfelt personal despair. Rhetorical exclamations, however, were common-place in the ancient world, and we should not assume they are necessarily authentic and personal cries from the heart. Paul has, in fact, for the purpose of the argument, put himself into the mind of the person who has failed to rely on the spirit of God. His purpose is to paint a vivid picture of the state of the person who is struggling to live by the resources of the flesh, as a striking contrast with the person who lives a life in the spirit, and who is described in the next chapter. Compare, incidentally, the use of the first person in 10.18, 19 and 11.1, where Paul is clearly expressing not his own thoughts but the thoughts of an opponent.

[14] The transition from 'we' to 'I' must be deliberate. Paul is deliberately putting himself forward as the main protagonist in this visualization.

'Fleshly', **sarkinos**, is used by Paul only three times. There is another word **sarkikos**, which he uses six times. Robinson follows Lightfoot's distinction, which he makes in his note on I Cor. 3.1, in suggesting that **sarkinos** is the morally neutral term meaning 'being in the flesh', while **sarkikos** denotes 'living according to the flesh', i.e. 'with the outlook of the flesh'. I am not persuaded that this distinction holds water, since Paul uses **sarkikos** in 15.27 in a morally neutral sense, and in I Cor. 3 **sarkinos** occurs in v. 1 and **sarkikos** in v. 3 with no obvious differentiation in meaning. In all these cases the Vulgate translates both words by *carnalis*.

'Sold to sin', **peprâmenos hypo tên hamartiân**, i.e. shipped off as a slave to serve sin. This verb is often used to denote exporting slaves and other merchandise in the course of trade.

[15] 'I do not know what I am doing' is said because things are happening over which I have no control. It does not mean, 'I do not know that what I am doing is wrong'.

[16] The argument of this verse is that the conflict between my moral sense and my desires, even though I finally give into temptation and commit a sin, proves that I agree with the Law which condemns the sin.

[17] Paul distinguishes between the inner core of self, which wants to act morally, and the sin which has taken control of the rest of the person.

[18] Because my real self, the inner core of my personality (see v. 22), is only free to *want* to do good, but not free actually to do it, the 'good' must have been driven out by sin.

'In my flesh' should be understood as meaning 'in my human nature', 'as a mere human being'. See my notes on Gal. 5.17 in *Reading through Galatians* for the significance of the term 'flesh' in Paul's letters.

[19] This verse adds an extra point to the previous verse: in the person living in the flesh sin not only prevents the self from doing good, but actually forces it to commit an evil act.

[20] A further point is made: when a person is so much under

the domination of sin that he does things which he does not want to do, he is no longer in control.

21 So I discover the law that, when I want to do good, I find evil available to me. 22 As regards the core of my personality, I take pleasure in God's Law, 23 but I see another law in my body which fights against the law of my mind and makes me its prisoner by the law of sin which is in my body. 24 What a pitiful creature I am! Who will rescue me from this body of death? 25 Thanks be to God through Jesus Christ our Lord! So then in my mind I serve personally the Law of God, but in my flesh [I serve] the law of sin.

[21–23] These are the conclusions reached from the previous argument: firstly, I am not free to do good, I am free only to do evil; secondly, there is an inner core of my personality which knows what is good and wants to do it; thirdly, in me the Law of God has been defeated by the law of sin, with the result that I am sin's slave.

'I find evil available to me', **emoi to kakon parakeitai**, literally, 'evil lies beside me', Vulg. *mihi malum adiacet*, NEB 'only the wrong is within my reach'. **Parakeitai** can also mean 'there is a choice', so we could paraphrase this sentence as 'the only choice I have is to do evil'.

'As regards the core of my personality', **kata ton esô anthrôpon**, literally, 'according to the inner man'.

Verse 23 is not easy to understand. There are not really three laws operating here, since the 'other' law is also 'the law of sin', which is referred to in v. 21 as 'the law that, when I want to do good, I find evil available to me', and can be defined as sin operating through the Mosaic Law, as described in vv. 5–11. Since it is 'the law of sin *which is in my body*', we could call it 'the law of the flesh'. In 8.2 it is called 'the law of sin and death'. On the other hand, 'the law of my mind' is 'the Law of God' of vv. 22 and 25, which includes, but is probably more than, the Mosaic Law in its spiritual aspect.

'Body', **melesin**, literally, 'limbs', is a synonym here for 'flesh'.

[24] 'Will rescue', **rhûsetai,** the same verb which occurs in the phrase '*deliver* us from evil' in the Lord's Prayer.

'This body of death', i.e. 'this body doomed to die', **tou sômatos tou thanatou toutou,** AV 'the body of this death'. The Vulg. *corpore mortis huius* can only be translated as 'the body of this death', but the Greek allows 'this' to go with 'body'.

[25] 'Thanks be to God through Jesus Christ our Lord!' should be taken as the answer to the preceding question expressed as one of those short praise formulae which are known to Jews as *berakoth*. In other words, it is an abbreviated way of saying, 'God will save me, for which thanks be to him through Jesus Christ our Lord'.

'Personally', **autos egô**, literally, 'I myself', i.e. in my inner core. Lightfoot suggests it means 'I by myself, I left alone, I without Christ', an interpretation supported by Robinson, but it reinforces the phrase 'in my mind' and is contrasted with 'in my flesh'. The point which Paul is making is that while we are still confined to our mortal bodies, they are subject to death and they are still sinful bodies. As he says in 8.10, 'If Christ is in you, your body is dead because of sin, but the spirit is life because of righteousness.' There is no need to suppose that the sentiment expressed in this verse can only be put forward by someone who is without Christ. Hence we should reject Lightfoot's and Robinson's interpretation.

Chapter 8

1 So then, [there is] no condemnation now for those in Christ Jesus. 2 For the Law of the spirit of life in Christ Jesus freed you from the law of sin and death. 3 For since the Law was powerless due to its weakness through the flesh, God sent his own son in the likeness of sinful flesh, and as a sin-offering condemned sin in the flesh, 4 so that the ordinance of the Law might be fulfilled in us when we walk according to the spirit and not according to the flesh.

[1] After painting the depressing picture of the state of mind of the 'fleshly' man, Paul now reassures his audience with a description of the 'spiritual' one who is in Christ. Note, incidentally, that the AV adds after 'in Christ Jesus' the words 'who walk not after the flesh, but after the spirit'. This is the reading of the text on which the AV was based, but it is not found in the majority of good manuscripts.

'There is no condemnation', because their sins have been forgiven, and, provided they remain in Christ, their sins will continue to be forgiven.

[2] 'The Law of the spirit of life in Christ Jesus' is a transformed and augmented version of 'the Law of God' of the previous chapter. As the 'spirit of life' it *gives* eternal life. As Sanday and Headlam say, it 'brings life because it

essentially *is* life.' In contrast, the Mosaic Law, which was in its essence 'holy, righteous and good', and acknowledged as such by the inner core of the person, was incapable of conquering sin or death. Because of the saving grace of Christ, God has produced a dynamic Law which has power to drive out 'the law of sin and death'. In Galatians, this dynamic Law is the covenant based on faith in Christ, or, as the writer of Hebrews describes it, the new and better covenant mediated by Jesus. It is noticeable that in Romans Paul is much more careful than he is in Galatians to avoid giving the impression that the Mosaic Law is to be completely scrapped.

[3] This verse makes a complex and subtle statement on the way Christ's sacrifice was effective against sin. The main point is that sin could only be defeated on its own ground, i.e. the flesh. God therefore makes his Son flesh in order to meet sin and defeat it. We do not know how this worked; all we are told is that this involved the sacrifice of Christ as a 'sin-offering'.

'Since the Law was powerless', **to adynaton tou nomou**, literally, 'the impossible of the Law', i.e. 'that which was impossible for the Law'.

'Due to its weakness through the flesh', in other words, 'because it was ineffectual operating through the medium of the flesh'.

'In the likeness' is not to be taken as 'like, but not really so', since that would imply that Jesus merely appeared to become a human being, as the Docetists claimed. Regarding 'likeness', see my note on Heb. 10.1 in *Reading through Hebrews*.

'Of sinful flesh' obviously does not mean that Jesus was sinful, but that he became human and so was incarnated in a body which had the potential for sin.

'As a sin-offering', **peri hamartiâs**, literally, 'for sin', is the technical term used in the OT in reference to the animals brought to the Temple for sacrifice. Note the hammer-like repetition of 'sin', **hamartiâ**, and 'flesh', **sarx**, in this verse, three times respectively.

[4] 'Ordinance', **dikaiôma**, NEB 'commandment'. This word carries many meanings. So far we have translated it as 'judgment', 'decree', 'justification' and 'act of justice'. As Paul is affirming the fulfilment of the Mosaic Law by the new Law of the spirit, the translation of this word must reflect the context of the Mosaic Law.

Walking 'according to the spirit', i.e. following the new Law of the spirit of life, is contrasted with walking 'according to the flesh', i.e. following the old Law of Moses; see below my notes on vv. 5 and 6.

5 For those who are in accord with the flesh think fleshly thoughts, but those who are in accord with the spirit [think] spiritual [thoughts]. 6 For fleshly thinking is death, but spiritual thinking is life and peace, 7 since fleshly thinking is hostility to God, as it is not subject to God's Law, nor can it be. 8 Those in the flesh cannot please God. 9 But you are in the spirit, not the flesh, if the spirit of God lives in you. And if anyone does not have Christ's spirit, he is not his.

[5, 6] These verses express a similar thought to that of Col. 3.2, 'Keep your minds on things above, not things on earth.'

'Fleshly thinking', **to phronêma tês sarkos**, can be contrasted with 'spiritual thinking', **to phronêma tou pneumatos**, in three obviously connected but still distinct areas:

1. having a materialistic attitude, being concerned exclusively and selfishly with the pursuit of such things as food, clothes, power, or money, instead of placing one's

gifts and resources at the service of God and other
human beings;

2. thinking of this world as the only one with which we
   need concern ourselves, taking an anthropocentric view,
   recognizing no religious dimension to life, instead of
   making one's relationship with God a priority, and
   seeing life in spiritual terms;

3. being concerned with the performing of rituals connected with the Mosaic Law, instead of relying on the
   grace of God and the power of the Holy Spirit with faith
   in Christ.

Commentators have tended to concentrate on the first two
categories when interpreting this verse, but the subject of this
and the previous passage is the position of the Law in the new
covenant, and so it most likely that Paul was referring to the
third category. 'Flesh' and 'spirit' are frequently contrasted by
Paul in passages where he is attacking those who are returning
to, or staying with, the ritual observances associated with the
Mosaic Law and can be illustrated by such passages as Gal.
3.2–3, 'Did you receive the Spirit from the works of the Law
or from a response to faith? Are you so senseless as to begin
with the Spirit and finish up now with the flesh?' and
Col.2.20–22, 'Why do you subject yourselves to ordinances
as though your life is in the world, "don't handle, don't taste,
don't touch", all things which are destined to be destroyed in
being used, according to the commandments and teachings of
human beings', and later in 14.17 of this letter, 'For the
kingdom of God is not food and drink, but righteousness,
peace and joy in the Holy Spirit'; see also Gal. 4.29 and Phil.
3.3.

[7] 'Fleshly thinking' is hostile to God because it will not and
cannot obey the spiritual commandments which are at the
core of God's Law. It is an enemy because it is a rebel.

[8, 9] Compare John 4.24, 'God is spirit and those who worship him must worship him in spirit and truth.' Since Christians have been given the spirit, they are enabled to worship and please God; although they are still physically 'in the flesh', they are also 'in the spirit'. Note that the spirit is closely identified with 'Christ's spirit', but, as Robinson says, 'this does not mean that Paul identifies the Spirit with Christ any more than he identifies Christ with the Father, though he can predicate the same functions and effects of each'.

'In the spirit', **en pneumati**, which the NEB waters down into 'on the spiritual level', while feebly paraphrasing 'not [in] the flesh' as 'But that is not how you live.'

10 If Christ [is] in you, your body is dead because of sin, but the spirit is life because of righteousness, 11 and if the spirit of the one who raised Jesus from the dead lives in you, he who raised Christ from the dead will make your mortal bodies alive too, through his spirit which lives in you. 12 So then, brothers and sisters, we are not under an obligation to the flesh to live according to its dictates. 13 For if you live according to the flesh, you will die, but if you kill the works of the body with the spirit, you will live.

[10] The antithesis in this verse is not quite symmetrical; we would have expected 'but your spirit is alive' to balance 'your body is dead'. Paul deliberately alters the antithesis to make it clear that we have no independent life or spirit of our own. The life which we have is the life of the spirit of God which is living in us. As he says in Gal. 2.20, 'I am no longer alive but Christ lives in me.'

'Your body is dead because of sin' seems to echo 7.9, 10, 'sin came alive and I died', and 7.11, 'for sin . . . killed me'. However, this is a more complex concept: 'body' has clearly been introduced as an antithesis to 'spirit', but there is another reason, as the next verse makes clear; the body is mortal, doomed to die, but will be resurrected by the power of the spirit. Just as we have died with Christ, so we will share in his bodily resurrection. We already have been resurrected spiritually, but as our bodies have not yet been resurrected, at the present time they must be dead. 'Because of sin', **dia hamartiân**, is also more complicated than it would appear at first sight, since, while sin brought spiritual death, and, as a result of Adam's sin, all human beings suffered physical death, there was another death which occurred when we died with Christ and were resurrected in baptism. This death, too, can be described as 'because of sin', since sin triggered off the process whereby we were saved by Christ's sacrifice. Käsemann seems to take **dia** as meaning something like 'with reference to', i.e. 'the body is dead so far as sin is in question', but such an interpretation is very doubtful. Furthermore, Paul would most probably have used the dative case **hamartiâi**, 'to sin', as in 6.2 and 6.10, if that were the meaning he had intended.

'Because of righteousness', or 'because of your justification'.

[11] Note how in this verse the spirit is referred to not as Christ's but God's, 'of the one who raised Jesus'.

'Will make . . . alive', **zôiöpoiêsei**, as Chrysostom observes, not just **anastêsei**, 'will raise', because everybody will be raised 'some for punishment, others to eternal life'.

'Through his spirit' is preferable to 'through the same spirit'.

[12] We are not under an obligation to sin but to something or someone else which is left unstated, i.e. the Spirit, according to Chrysostom, as the emphasis in the original word order makes clear, 'we are debtors not to the flesh'.

'According to its dictates', literally, 'according to the flesh'.

[13] 'You will die', **mellete apothnêiskein**, is not a simple statement of a future event, but rather a warning that death will be the result if you go on behaving like that. **Mellô** often means 'I intend' or 'it is likely that I will'.

'The works of the body', **tâs prâxeis tou sômatos**, are virtually identical with 'the works of the flesh' here. **Prâxis** is a rare word in the NT and in Paul's letters found only here, in 12.4, and in Col. 3.9, 'you have put off the old man *along with his deeds* (**syn tais prâxesin autou**)'.

14 For those who are driven by the spirit of God are the sons and daughters of God. 15 For you did not receive a spirit which enslaved you again to fear, but a Spirit which adopted you as sons and daughters, through which we [can] cry out 'Abba, Father!' 16 The Spirit itself bears witness along with our spirit that we are the children of God. 17 If we are children, [we are] also heirs, heirs of God and joint heirs with Christ, if we suffer along with him in order to be glorified also along with him.

[14] 'Are driven', **agontai**, rather than 'are led' (AV), as in Gal. 5.18, 'If you are driven by the spirit, you are not under the Law', a more dynamic relationship.

'Sons and daughters' is represented by the one word **huîoi**, 'sons', which was never meant to be an exclusive term. Paul adds the phrase 'and daughters' in II Cor. 6.18, 'and I will be as a Father to you, and you will be to me as sons and *daughters* (**thygateras**)'. The phrase 'children of God', **tekna Theou**, of v. 16 has at least the advantage of being neuter. Although we can be called 'sons of God' because we follow God's commandments, or because we have been created in his image, or even because we only become truly such in the next world, the sense Paul intends here is that we are adopted as brothers and sisters of Jesus, and hence become the sons and daughters of God, when we receive the Holy Spirit at baptism. This is made clearer in the next verse.

[15] This and the next two verses express the same thoughts as those in Gal. 4.6, 7, 'And because you are sons, God has sent out into our hearts his son's spirit which cries out "Abba (that is, Father)!" So you are no longer a slave but a son, and if a son, then you are also an heir through God.'

'A spirit which enslaved you again to fear', i.e. which forced you to observe again the Mosaic Law. The word 'again' clearly refers to a previous state of slavery, and the association of 'fear' with observance of the old covenant is illustrated in Heb. 12.18–23, where the gloom and terror of Sinai, representing the old covenant, is dramatically contrasted with the joy of Sion, which stands for the new covenant. Paul is clearly addressing former Jews or Gentile converts to Judaism.

'A Spirit which adopted you as sons and daughters', **pneuma huîothesiâs**, literally, 'spirit of adoption'.

[16] Käsemann points out that 'our spirit' is not our 'inner life', but the spirit of the community of Christian worshippers who can confidently address God as 'Father'. I would go further: we know we are the children of God because we exhibit the gifts of the Holy Spirit; it is not just a feeling of assurance inside us, nor merely our communal acclamation of God as 'Father', but our visible powers which prove who we are.

[17] 'Heirs', **klêronomoi**, are by definition people who do not yet enjoy their inheritance. So, although we are already children of God, we have not yet entered into full possession of what has been promised to us.

'Joint heirs', **syngklêronomoi**, a word found only four times in the NT, is used in Eph. 3.6 to describe the Gentiles who are 'joint heirs' with the Jews of the promise in Christ. Here we are all 'joint heirs' with Christ. This does not mean that Christ has not yet entered into his inheritance, but that we, too, will share the inheritance which he already enjoys. The sign of that inheritance is glorification. Note also that it is conditional – 'if we *suffer along with* him (**sympaschomen**) in order to *be glorified* also *along with* him (**syndoxasthômen**)'. The repetition of **syn-** compounds is typical of Paul; compare Col. 2.12, 13; Eph. 2.6 and 3.6.

18 For I reckon that the sufferings of the present time are not worthy of comparison with the glory which is going to be revealed for us. 19 For creation awaits with eager longing the revelation of the sons and daughters of God. 20 For creation was subjected to futility, not willingly, but because of the one who subjected it, in hope, 21 since creation itself shall also be liberated from the slavery of destruction into the freedom of the glory of the children of God. 22 For we know that the whole of creation has been groaning and sharing birth pains together up to the present; 23 and not only [creation], but even ourselves, who actually possess the first fruits of the Spirit, yes, we, too, groan inwardly as we await our adoption, the redemption of our bodies.

[18] 'For us', **eis hêmâs**, i.e. 'in store for us' (NEB) or, as the AV has it, 'in us', Vulg. *in nobis*.

[19] 'Creation awaits with eager longing', literally, 'the earnest expectation of creation awaits'. While the word translated

as 'creation', **ktisis**, can sometimes mean 'creature', as the AV has it, it probably refers here and in the next verse to the whole of creation. Jerome does not favour this interpretation and seems to support the view that Paul is referring to the angels and ourselves, while noting that some believe that he is referring to Adam and Eve. The AV, incidentally, translates this word as 'creation' in v. 22. The notion that the world itself will be renewed and transformed at the end of time is found also in Rev. 21.1, 'And I saw a new heaven and a new earth. For the first heaven and the first earth vanished, and the sea no longer existed.'

[20] 'Creation was subjected to futility', **têi mataiotêti hê ktisis hypetagê**, means 'the material world was subject to death and decay'; in other words, it was doomed to impermanence. The clue to this interpretation can be found in Eccles. 1.2 (Sept.), ' "Vanity of vanities", said the preacher, "vanity of vanities, everything is vanity" ', where the word 'vanity' translates **mataiotês**, the word used here by Paul. The Ecclesiastes passage goes on to give examples of the futility of life, and the repeated cycle of coming into being and passing away in the natural world. This is clearly the sense intended here.

'Not willingly' does not imply that the natural world has a will of its own, and that it was forced to accept this subjection to futility, but rather that it had no choice in the matter. It is irrelevant to ask if it has a will or not. The emphasis here is on the necessity of the process, not the unwillingness of the created world.

'The one who subjected' is God, rather than Adam or Satan. Sanday and Headlam suggest that it refers to the occasion when God passed sentence on Adam and Eve and their descendants after the Fall.

'In hope' refers back to the 'eager longing' of the previous verse. It may strike one as odd that Paul attributes personality

and sentience to creation, but the material world includes
animals, and we find in the OT even the inanimate parts of
creation described as though they were capable of expressing
themselves: for example, Ps. 148. 7-9 (AV), 'Praise the Lord
from the earth, ye dragons, and all deeps: fire, and hail; snow,
and vapour; stormy wind fulfilling his word: mountains, and
all hills; fruitful trees, and all cedars.'

[21] 'Also', i.e. besides human beings. This shows that
'creation itself' must denote the non-human world.

'The slavery of destruction', **tês douleiâs tês phthorâs**, in
other words, 'the inevitability of death and decay' or, as the
NEB says, 'the shackles of mortality'. This is strangely
reminiscent, although one should not push the similarity too
far, of the Buddhist doctrine of the cycle of existence.

'Freedom of the glory' is more than the AV 'glorious
liberty'; it is both glory and freedom, but freedom defined as
liberation from the inevitability of death, in other words,
eternal life.

[22] This verse testifies to the solidarity and unity of creation
and the fact that salvation is not limited to humanity. Adam's
fall, through his headship over and involvement with the
created world, affected creation. The whole of the universe
suffers together, not necessarily with us in this verse, since we
are referred to separately in the next verse.

'Has been groaning and sharing birth pains together',
systenazei kai synôdînei, a pair of **syn-** compounds found
nowhere else in the NT. Paul uses the simple verb **ôdînô**, 'I am
in travail', metaphorically in Gal. 4.19, but the most interesting parallel is in Mark 13.8 (compare also Matt. 24.7, 8),
where Jesus seems to speak of the world suffering birth pains
as the end approaches, 'and there will be earthquakes in
places, there will be famines; these are the start of the *birth
pains* (**ôdînôn**)'. Note that I have translated the present as a

past continuous tense; see my note on 1.20 on this special usage denoting an action which took place in the past and is still taking place.

'Up to the present', **achri tou nûn**, i.e. 'and is still doing so'.

[23] 'Even ourselves', **kai autoi**, is reinforced by 'yes, we, too', **hêmeis kai autoi**; Paul emphasizes the fact that even Christians groan and suffer as they await their final redemption, in spite of enjoying the gift of the Holy Spirit.

'First fruits', **aparchên**, is not exactly a 'deposit on a purchase', as Käsemann says. To put it more accurately, it is the advance on our inheritance, a foretaste of the banquet. **Aparchê** can also mean 'birth certificate', but that is not the sense it has here. In Eph. 1.14 the Holy Spirit is described as a 'down payment of our inheritance', **arrabôn tês klêronomiâs**, which is another metaphor expressing the same idea.

'Inwardly', **en heautois**, literally, 'in ourselves', which could also mean 'among ourselves'.

'As we await our adoption', **huîothesiân apekdechomenoi**, would appear to contradict Paul's earlier statement (vv. 14–16) that we were adopted before and are already sons and daughters of God. There is, in fact, no contradiction; as there are two stages in our redemption, the first being our initial purchase and liberation from sin by Christ's sacrifice (3.24), and the second being the 'redemption of our bodies' when we are resurrected at the end, so there are two stages in our adoption which correspond to these. It is interesting that the Greek has a singular 'redemption of our *body* (**sômatos**)', but we should not read too much into this; it does not mean here the body of Christ, i.e. the church, but the individual body of each one of us. Paul is equally inexact about number when referring to 'hearts' or 'minds'.

We should not be surprised if Paul uses the term 'redemption' in more than one sense. For instance, in Eph. 1.14, quoted above, he goes on to speak of 'the redemption of our acquisition' in regard to our finally taking possession of our inheritance; in other words, it refers not to us being redeemed, but to us redeeming our property. Could 'redemption of our bodies' here refer to us coming into possession of our new, glorious bodies, or does it refer to God finally releasing our bodies from the sphere of sin and death? Whichever option we go for, the idea of payment is still at the core of the word 'redemption': the payment has already been paid by Christ, but the final release of our bodies from the slavery of death has not yet been achieved.

24 For we were saved by hope; but hope that can be seen is not hope. For who hopes for something he can see? 25 If we hope for something we cannot see, we wait for it with patience. 26 Similarly, the Spirit, too, helps us in our weakness; for we do not know what to pray for in the way that we should, but the Spirit itself pleads [for us] with silent groans. 27 He who searches out the hearts knows the mind of the Spirit because it intercedes for the saints in accordance with God.

[24] 'Hope' is closely identified with 'faith', since both depend on perseverance in the face of difficulties and on steadfast obedience even when there seems to be little reason to believe or hope. As Heb. 11.27 says of Moses, 'By faith he left Egypt unafraid of the king's anger; for he persevered as though he saw the unseen one.' The connection between faith and hope is made explicit in Heb. 11.1, 'Faith is the foundation of our hopes, the argument for invisible things.' The obvious difference between them is that hope looks forward, while faith operates in the present, but this distinction is often blurred, as we discover when we look at the examples of faith in chapter 11 of Hebrews. **Elpis** is a much stronger word than than our word 'hope', as Chrysostom

says: 'it is having confidence in the future', **to tois mellousi tharrhein**. We tend to use 'I hope' when we mean 'I wish that it would happen', but the meaning of the verb in Greek is closer to 'I expect', 'I look forward to'. It can also be used in reference to evil things to mean 'I fear'. Several commentators have problems with the idea that we can be saved *by* hope, and translate the word **elpidi**, the dative case of **elpis**, in various ways, e.g. '*though only in* hope' (NEB), and '*with this* hope *in view*' (Moffatt). There is, however, no real problem since Eph. 2.5, 'by grace you have been saved', and Eph. 2.8, 'you have been saved by grace through faith', provide us with the context for interpreting Paul's statement here; our salvation was an act of grace on God's part, since we did not deserve it, but it is only realized when we have faith and hope. Hope is as necessary as faith, since faith without hope is no faith at all. In other words, hope and faith together enable us to receive the salvation which was presented to us by grace. We should remember that hope is important enough to be ranked with faith and love in I Cor. 13.13, 'And there now remain these three, faith, hope and love', and when Paul goes on to say 'but the greatest of these is love', I do not recall him adding, 'and hope is the least important of the three'.

'For who hopes for something he can see?', **ho gar blepei tis elpizei**, is probably the best reading of the text. There is a reading which gives **ho gar blepei tis, ti kai elpizei**, hence the AV 'for what a man seeth, why doth he yet hope for?' The NEB 'why should a man endure and wait for what he already sees' is based on yet another text which has **hypomenei**, 'endures', instead of **elpizei**, 'hopes for'. There are also other variant readings, but it would take too long to go into them in greater detail.

[25] The point here seems to be that we become patient through waiting in hope.

[26] 'Helps', **synantilambanetai**, is only found in the NT here and in Luke 10.40.

'Pleads', **hyperentyngchanei**, found nowhere else in the NT, is a compound of the verb **entyngchanô**, which Paul uses in the next verse.

'Silent groans', **stenagmois alalêtois**, Vulg. *gemitibus inenarrabilibus*, not 'wordless sighs', or anything else which human beings can hear. It has been fashionable to interpret this phrase as some manifestation of glossolalia, but **alalêtois** means literally 'unspoken', 'unspeakable', or even 'not to be spoken', which is close to the Latin *inenarrabilibus*. Käsemann's translator renders it as 'inexpressible sighs', which seems to be self-contradictory. If they are inexpressible they cannot be expressed, but Käsemann goes on to say they are heard in worship and therefore they must have been expressed. Paul is surely making the point that the Holy Spirit pleads for us without our knowledge and silently. Käsemann has some support for his statement that Paul 'is speaking with reference to certain practices in congregational life' from Chrysostom who defines the Spirit here as 'the Spirit of prayer' and states that in apostolic times people with this gift used to pray for the whole congregation, rather like the deacon did in his time. But Chrysostom describes the groans as 'in the mind', **kata dianoiân**. A determination to interpret this phrase as referring to human utterances led the authors of the NEB to translate it as 'through our inarticulate groans', although 'our' cannot be extracted from the original Greek, nor can **alalêtois** mean 'inarticulate', a word normally used to describe something spoken indistinctly, i.e. an utterance consisting of sounds which do not resemble words.

I believe that there are two things happening here: firstly, the human being is praying and uttering audible groans, and secondly, the Holy Spirit is accompanying him with inaudible groans, which only God can hear. It should be noted that Jesus also makes intercession for his church according to Heb.

7.25, 'since he lives for ever *in order to plead* (**eis to entyngchanein**) for them'. Clearly, Jesus can plead directly to his Father, not only through the mouths of his followers. Käsemann, however, clearly thinks that the Holy Spirit is different, since he 'does his work, *intercession included*, in the sphere and through the ministry of the community'.

'[For us]', **hyper hêmôn**, is found in some manuscripts, but it is not necessary for the sense.

[27] 'He who searches out the hearts', i.e. God.

'In accordance with God', **kata Theon**, i.e. according to God's will. Hence, as the intercession of the Holy Spirit is what God wishes, God knows the intention of the intercession. Furthermore, the implication is that God will grant such requests.

28 We know that, for those who love God, those who have been called according to his purpose, everything works together for good, 29 since those whom he knew beforehand he also ordained beforehand should share the form of his son's likeness, so that he might be the first-born among many brethren. 30 Those whom he ordained beforehand he also called, and those whom he called he also justified, and those whom he justified he also glorified.

[28] 'Everything works together for good', **panta synergei eis agathon**, could also be translated, 'He works everything together for good'. Some manuscripts have the additional reading **ho Theos**, 'God', which supports the latter translation. It looks, however, as though 'God' was added as a gloss to provide a personal subject for the verb. There is no need to assume that this verb cannot have 'everything' as its subject, since in James 2.22 it has 'faith' as its subject. The NEB makes

the Holy Spirit the subject by linking this verse with the previous verse and translating, 'and in everything, as we know, he co-operates for good with those who love God'.

[29] This verse is echoed by Eph. 1.5, 'having ordained us beforehand for adoption by him through Jesus Christ', and makes the same point, i.e. that God only makes us his children by adoption through our relationship with his first-born son, Jesus Christ. For 'knew beforehand' see the notes on 11.2.

'Share the form of his son's likeness', **symmorphous tês eikonos tou huiou autou**, is a complex idea: does it refer to taking on the form of his resurrected or his earthly body? Phil. 3.21 says that Christ will change 'the body of our humility, [making it to] *share form* (**symmorphon**) with the body of his glory'. Clearly this reference is to our future resurrected state. But the process of transformation starts when we are baptized into Christ and continues, as II Cor. 3.18 suggests, 'as we mirror the glory of the Lord *we are changed into the same likeness* (**tên autên eikona metamorphoumetha**) from glory into glory'. We can reject the idea that our share in the 'form of his son's likeness' merely refers to our visible and physical likeness to God, or rather to Christ who bears a human form. Even unredeemed man still bears that image which comes from our creation in the image of God, whereas this invisible and spiritual likeness is one that can only be shared by those who have a special relationship with Christ.

'First-born', **prôtotokon**, is used here to make the point that God intended that his first-born son should not be his only son, but the eldest of a series of sons and daughters. Colossians 1.18, 'first-born from the dead' makes a similar point, i.e. that Christ was intended to be the first of a series of sons who will be resurrected.

[30] 'He glorified', **edoxasen**, is aorist, a tense which is used when referring to an event in the past, but is also used to

describe timeless activity. Strictly speaking we are not yet glorified but, as I point out in the previous verse, the process has already started, even though it is not obvious.

Many scholars have discussed the problem of predestination when commenting on this passage, but as it is not necessary for an understanding of the meaning I will pass on.

31 What shall we say then in regard to this? If God is for us, who is against us? 32 How will he, who did not spare his own son but surrendered him for all of us, not lavish on us everything along with him? 33 Who will accuse God's chosen ones? God, the one who justifies us? 34 Who is our condemner? Christ, the one who died, or rather who was raised up, who is even on the right hand of God, who is also pleading for us? 35 Who will separate us from the love of Christ? Affliction or distress, persecution or hunger, nakedness, danger, the sword? 36 As it is written, 'For your sake we are put to death all day, we have been reckoned to be sheep for slaughter.' 37 But in all these things we are more than victorious through the one who loved us. 38 For I am persuaded that neither death nor life, neither angels nor rulers, neither the present nor the future, nor powers, 39 nor height, depth or any other creature will be able to separate us from the love of God which is in Christ Jesus our Lord.

[31] Paul now sums up this section with one of the most moving passages which he ever wrote, so moving, in fact, that some have been tempted to call it a hymn. But we should not lose sight of the main purpose of this passage, which is to

reassure his audience that by putting their trust in the new covenant of Christ they can safely give up their observance of the Mosaic Law.

'In regard to this', **pros tauta**, not 'against this'.

[32] 'Surrendered', **paredôken**, is frequently used in reference to Christ being given up in sacrifice. In Romans it is God who surrenders his son, whereas in Galatians (2.20) and Ephesians (5.2, 25) it is Christ who surrenders himself.

'Will lavish', **charisetai**, from **charizomai**, a verb related to word **charis**, 'grace'. See my notes in *Reading through Colossians and Ephesians* on Col. 2.13 regarding the various meanings of this verb.

'Everything along with him', i.e. in addition to giving up his son on our behalf God will give us everything else. It is less likely that 'along with him', **syn autôi**, means 'in fellowship with him'.

[33, 34] These rhetorical questions may have been suggested by, but, despite Robinson's claim that they are a quotation, are hardly based on, Isa. 50.8 (Sept.): 'The one who justified me is near. Who is the one who gives judgment on me? Let him stand forth at once against me. And who is the one who gives judgment on me? Let him come near me.' I have followed Barrett in treating them all as questions, not just those beginning with 'who'. The AV and NEB both treat the sentences beginning with 'God' and 'Christ' respectively as statements (although the NEB in a marginal note seems to admit the possibility that these also are questions) and, as a result, lose the force and irony of the rhetorical questions and create statements which imply that God *will* accuse us and that Christ *will* condemn us. Paul is pointing out how ridiculous it is to imagine that God, who has forgiven us, could accuse us, and that Christ, who is actually pleading for us in heaven, could condemn us.

'Even', **kai**, is omitted by some manuscripts.

[35] Another pair of questions, translated as such this time by both the AV and NEB.

'Affliction', **thlîpsis**, and 'distress', **stenochôriâ**, occur as a pair in 2.9. See the notes on that verse.

'Sword', i.e. the executioner's sword.

[36] This quotation comes from Ps. 44.22 (Sept. 43.23).

[37] 'We are more than victorious', **hypernîkômen**, occurs nowhere else in the NT.

[38] Because 'rulers', **archai**, are associated with 'angels' it is likely that Paul is referring to supernatural powers. 'Powers', **dynameis**, is also a word used with **archai** in Eph. 1.21 in a list of supernatural authorities, but it could also refer to earthly ones as well. In the light of what Paul goes on to mention in the next verse, there is a strong probability that he is referring to the forces who rule the stars and planets.

[39] 'Height', **hypsôma**, is not the normal word for height and, as Käsemann and Barclay point out, is a technical term used in astrology. It denotes the elevation or exaltation of a heavenly body in a sign of the zodiac. 'Depth', **bathos**, is the term for the dejection of a planet, i.e. when it is in the sign opposite to that in which it is exalted.

'The love of God which is in Christ Jesus' has at least two meanings: it is the love which God demonstrated by the incarnation and sacrifice of his son and it is also the same love which Christ shows to us.

Chapter 9

1 I am speaking the truth in Christ – I am not lying – and my conscience bears witness with me in the Holy Spirit, [when I say] 2 that I feel great grief and unremitting pain in my heart. 3 For I would pray to be cast out myself from Christ for the sake of my brethren, my kinsmen according to the flesh, 4 who are the people of Israel, to whom belong the adoption, the glory, the covenants, the gift of the Law, the worship and the promises, 5 to whom belong the patriarchs, and from whom the Christ [came] according to the flesh – [may] the God who is above all things [be] blessed for ever, amen.

This and the next two chapters are on a single theme: the place of Israel in God's plan of redemption. The fact that these chapters hang together and display a unity of structure has led some commentators to call them an excursus, even an interpolation, but they form an integral part of Paul's argument.

[1, 2] The painful emotions expressed in these verses are almost tangible. The opening reminds one of another place where Paul shows his personal feelings, i.e. Gal.1.20, 'Look here, before God, what I am writing to you is no lie.'

[3] Paul is saying here that, if it could save his fellow Jews, he would be prepared to give up his own salvation. This protestation is most probably meant to counter the stories that Paul, the apostle to the Gentiles, had turned his back on his people, as Acts 21.28 says about the Asiatic Jews who caught sight of Paul in the Temple in Jerusalem and shouted, 'Men of Israel, help! This is the man whose teaching to everybody everywhere is against his people, the Law and this place.'

'Cast out', **anathema**: see my notes on Gal. 1.8, 9 in *Reading through Galatians*.

[4] 'The people of Israel', literally 'Israelites': this word is rarely used by Paul, and only when he is referring to the special relationship which the Jews had with God.

'Adoption', **huîothesiâ**, in the previous chapter was used to describe the new relationship as a son of God which is conferred by becoming a brother of Christ. Here it denotes the older concept of the Jews as the children of Israel, which is referred to in Deut. 14.1 (Sept.), 'You are the sons of the Lord your God', and Ex. 4.22 (Sept.), 'Israel is my first-born son'.

'Glory', **doxa**, has generally been taken as referring to those occasions in Jewish history when God revealed his glory. For example, Ex. 24.17 (Sept.) speaks of the glory of God on Mount Sinai, 'And the appearance of the glory of the Lord was like a blazing fire on the crest of the mountain facing the children of Israel.' It is odd, however, to speak of this glory, which is clearly God's, as belonging to the Israelites, and it is possible that **doxa** here carries the very common meaning 'reputation' or 'fame', since the Jews were famous for their religious beliefs and practices.

'Covenants' is singular in some manuscripts, probably because their scribes would have remembered only one covenant, the one made with Moses on Sinai. There were, however, more than one; some early scholars could recall

four: the first with Noah, the second with Abraham, the third
with Moses and the fourth the new covenant in Christ. Barrett
lists the covenants with Adam, Noah, Abraham and Moses,
but also suggests that Paul is thinking of the separate
covenants which God made with Moses during the Exodus
of the Israelites.

'Gift of the Law', **nomothesiâ**, and 'worship', **latreiâ**, are
connected, because the rules for the worship of God were laid
down in the Mosaic code.

The 'promises', **epangeliai**, are probably those given to
Abraham but may include all the messianic promises, since
the next verse refers to the Messiah.

[5] 'Patriarchs', **pateres**, literally, 'fathers'.

'The Christ', **ho Christos**, as the unusual use of the definite
article shows, is 'the Anointed one', i.e. the Messiah. 'According to the flesh' refers to the fact that he was an Israelite
through his mother. Clearly, Paul is implying that his father
'according to the spirit' was God.

'[May] the God who is above all things [be] blessed for
ever', **ho ôn epi pantôn Theos eulogêtos eis tous aiônas**, can
be taken with the previous clause and translated, as the AV
does, as 'who is over all, God blessed for ever'. Clearly, the
AV takes 'God' as referring to Christ; if correct, this is the
only case of Paul directly addressing Christ as God. Commentators have taken up theological positions on this crux, but
our obligation is to establish without prejudice what Paul
actually meant. We can be pretty sure that Paul would have
agreed with Thomas, who said to the risen Christ 'My Lord
and my God', and we can infer from much of Paul's writing
that he believed in the divinity of Christ, but the fact is that in
his letters he avoids actually calling Jesus 'God', and the term
'God above all' is even less likely to be found in Paul as an
epithet of Christ. Grammatically speaking there is little to
choose between the two versions. The omission of the verb

'may he be' in the original is not an argument for rejecting the version I have chosen, since such an omission is so common in Greek that it passes unnoticed (see Eph.1.3). Stylistically speaking, a doxology directed to the Father is much more likely than one directed to the Son. The standard short praise formula is found in 1.25, 'Who exchanged the truth of God for falsehood, and who worshipped and revered the creature rather than the creator, *who is blessed for ever* (**hos estin eulogêtos eis tous aiônas**), amen.' A closer parallel is found in II Cor. 11.31, 'The God and Father of our Lord Jesus knows, *he who is blessed for ever* (**ho ôn eulogêtos eis tous aiônas**), that I do not lie.' In both these cases it is the Father who is blessed. Commentators have suggested other ways out of this impasse, such as putting a stop after 'all' and translating 'who is over all. May God be blessed for ever', and some have even emended the text from **ho ôn** to **hôn ho**, to produce the reading '*to whom belongs* the God above all, blessed for ever'. Neither of these last two suggestions carries much weight, and we are left with a straight choice between the two previous interpretations.

6 It is not as though the word of God has failed; for not all those who are [descended] from Israel [are] Israel, 7 nor [are they] all [his] children because [they are the] seed of Abraham, but 'in Isaac shall your seed be called'. 8 That is, [it is] not the children of the flesh [who are the] children of God, but the children of the promise [who] are reckoned as the seed. 9 For this is what is said about the promise, 'at this time I will come and Sarah will have a son'.

[6] 'It is not as though', **ouch hoion de hoti**, is an idiom which the NEB 'it is impossible that' mistranslates. The Vulg. *non autem quod* and the AV 'not as though' are correct. As there is

not a single case in the NT of **hoios** meaning 'possible', **ouch hoion** cannot mean 'impossible'.

'The word of God' refers to the promises of God as recorded in scripture. Sanday and Headlam gloss it as 'the declared purpose of God'.

'From Israel', i.e. descended from Abraham's grandson Jacob, who was renamed Israel when God appeared to Jacob. The Genesis passage which underpins this statement is 35.10, 11 (Sept.), 'And God said to him, "Your name shall no longer be called Jacob, but Israel will be your name . . . I am your God; increase and multiply. There will be nations and companies of nations from you, and kings shall come forth from your loins." ' Since the word 'nations', **ethnê**, can also be translated as 'the Gentiles', this text is particularly relevant to Paul's argument.

[7–8] The argument of these verses is very condensed. Paul is saying here that descent from Abraham does not make one a son of God, or a true son of Abraham, since the promise given to Abraham and his seed only operates through the covenant which God made with his son Isaac even before he was born (Gen. 17.19, 21), and, what is more important, this promise is only valid for those who are justified by faith. In other words, it is not physical descent, i.e. being 'children of the flesh', but a spiritual affinity, being 'children of the promise', which makes one an heir of the promise, as he has already hinted in 4.13, 'For the promise that he should inherit the world [was] not [given] to Abraham or his seed through the Law but through justification by faith.' In Gal. 3.16 Paul actually restricts the title 'seed of Abraham' to Christ, in order to make it even clearer that mere physical descent from Abraham is not a qualification for receiving the promise.

'[His]' has to be added, but the question remains: whose children are they? Israel's, Abraham's or God's? Several commentators think they are Abraham's, but I believe Paul is still talking about God's children, since he continues to speak of these in the next verse. It is not, however, crucial to the argument to establish whose children they are, since Abraham's true children, i.e. those who are his spiritual descendants, are also God's, as Gal. 3.29 says, 'If you are Christ's, then you are Abraham's seed, heirs according to the promise.'

'In Isaac shall your seed be called' comes from Gen. 21.12, a passage in which God tells Abraham to expel Ishmael his son by Hagar.

[9] The quotation is loosely based on a combination of Gen. 18.10 and 14 (Sept.).

'For this is what is said about the promise', literally, 'for this [is] the word of the promise', makes it clear that the promise operated through Sarah's son, and not Hagar's.

10 And not only this, but also [there is the case of] Rebecca, when she was pregnant from one man, Isaac our father. 11 For, at a time when [her children] had not yet been born and had not yet done anything, either good or bad, in order that the purpose of God in regard to choice should stand 12 not as the result of deeds but as coming from the one who calls, it was said to her, 'The elder shall serve the younger.' 13 As it is written, 'I loved Jacob and hated Esau.'

[10] Rebecca was carrying twins, Jacob and Esau, at the time God spoke to her. The first to be born was Esau, which would normally have made him the heir of the promise which had been given originally to Abraham and passed on to Isaac, as described in Gen. 26.3, 4. The main point, however, of God's rejection of Esau in favour of Jacob is not to demonstrate the physical line of descent from Abraham through Jacob, but to establish the fact that God is the one who determines who

should be his children, not the mechanical operation of the laws of primogeniture. As Dodd says, 'It is for Him to decide with absolute freedom who shall constitute that chosen people.'

[11] 'The purpose in regard to choice', **hê kat'eklogên prothesis**, NEB 'selective purpose', which echoes 8.28, 'those who have been called *according to his purpose* (**kata prothesin**)', emphasizes God's freedom to choose whom he wishes.

[12] 'Not as the result of deeds but as coming from the one who calls', literally, 'not from deeds but from the one calling', should be taken with the previous clause rather than the following 'it was said'. It picks up the earlier reference to the fact that the twins had not yet done anything. In other words, neither of them had earned favour or disfavour from God as a result of their actions. 'The one who calls', i.e. God, is the one who decides who shall be chosen.

'The elder shall serve the younger' comes from Gen. 25.23.

[13] This quotation is from Mal. 1.2, 3, and should not be taken too literally. It is a strong idiom for the milder 'I preferred Jacob to Esau'.

14 So what shall we say? Surely there is no injustice with God? Heaven forbid! 15 For he says to Moses, 'I will show mercy to whomsoever I show mercy, and I will pity whomsoever I pity.' 16 So, then, [it depends] not on someone's will or performance, but on God's mercy. 17 For the scripture says to Pharaoh, 'For this reason I raised you up, in order to demonstrate my power in dealing with you and so that my name might be proclaimed in the whole

earth.' 18 So, then, he has mercy on whom he wishes [to have mercy], and stiffens whom he wishes [to stiffen].

[14] If God decides who will be saved, it might be objected that this is unfair. Paul goes on to answer this objection by reinforcing the statement of v. 11, namely, that the choice is God's.

[15] This quotation comes from Ex. 33.19 (Sept.) and occurs in a passage where God grants Moses' request to see his glory.

[16] To paraphrase this verse: everything is in the hands of God, and the fact that someone wants a particular outcome, as Moses did, or has done or not done something to deserve it, as in the case of Esau and Jacob who had done nothing because they were not yet born, is irrelevant. God will show mercy as he thinks fit.

'Performance', **trechontos**, literally, 'running', a metaphor also used by Paul elsewhere, e.g. Gal. 2.2, 'in case *I was labouring* (**trechô**) or had laboured in vain', and Gal. 5.7, 'you were making good progress', **etrechete kalôs**.

[17] This is from Ex. 9.16 (Sept.), but the variations in vocabulary and grammar in the first part of the verse indicate that Paul is quoting from memory and, in part, probably from the original Hebrew. For example, instead of 'I raised you up' the Septuagint has 'you were preserved', and the word for 'power', **dynamin**, has supplanted the original **ischyn**, 'strength'.

'I raised you up', i.e. 'I gave you your powerful position'.

[18] God showed mercy to Moses and the Israelites and stiffened, i.e. made stubborn, Pharaoh.

19 Then you will say to me, 'So why does he still assign blame? For who withstands his will?' 20 On the contrary, man, who are you to answer God back? 'Surely the pot will not say to the potter, "Why did you make me like this?"' 21 Does the potter not have power over the clay to make from the same lump one vessel for honour and another for dishonour? 22 And what if God, in his great patience, put up with the vessels of wrath which have been made fit for destruction, because he wished to demonstrate his wrath and to make known his power, 23 and in order to make known the treasures of his glory over the vessels of mercy which he prepared beforehand for glory? 24 These, indeed, are us, whom he called not only from the Jews but also from the Gentiles.

[19] The point which the objector is making by asking the rhetorical question 'For who withstands his will?' is that nobody has the power to do anything which God does not wish, and therefore, if he does something wicked, he cannot be blamed because he has only done what God allowed him to do.

'Withstands', **anthestêken**, a perfect tense with a present sense.

[20] The quotation is a condensed version of Isa. 29.16 (Sept.), which, instead of "Why did you make me like this?", in the original reads, "Did you not make me?", and continues, 'Or shall the thing made say to its maker, "You did not make me skilfully"?' Compare also Isa. 45.9. The potter and his clay as allegories of God and his creation occur in various parts of the OT.

'On the contrary', **menounge**, AV 'nay but', which is used only by Paul in the NT, introduces a remark intended to correct a previous statement. Paul is saying in effect to the objector, 'Are you asking God questions? Don't be ridiculous! He is the one who asks the questions.'

[21] This time the allegory seems to be suggested by more than one passage, Jer. 18. 1–11, where the potter who remakes a pot when it is turning out badly is a metaphor for God doing what he likes with Israel, and Wisdom 15.7, where the potter makes different vessels for different purposes from the same clay, as he sees fit.

[22–24] These verses are not easy to understand. The meaning hinges on our interpretation of the word **thelôn** in v. 22, literally, 'wishing'. At first sight it seems better to take this present participle as a concessive '*although* he wished', as Sanday and Headlam suggest, but a causal meaning, '*because* he wished', is more appropriate. The emphasis is on 'he put up with' and 'in his great patience'. God could have abandoned the people of Israel as being impossible to amend, since they always let him down, but he tolerated their shortcomings in order to prepare the ground for the revelation of his great plan for the salvation of the whole world through his son. We are reminded of Paul's earlier argument that there had to be a period when sin seemed to triumph so that God's grace might have more effect. For example, 5.20, 'The Law came in so that the transgression might be in excess; and where sin was in excess, grace was super-abundant.' So, because God wished to make his righteousness manifest by the judgment he would mete out to the 'vessels of wrath', he gave them, as we might say, 'enough rope to hang themselves' and also, incidentally, enough time to repent. This set the stage for the exercise of the other aspect of God's righteousness, the justification of sinners by the sacrifice of his own son.

'Vessels of wrath' and 'vessels of mercy' continue the

metaphor of the potter and his pots. The former are those who
deserve to receive wrath, i.e. be punished, the latter those on
whom God will show mercy (not those who deserve mercy,
since nobody deserves that). Chrysostom, wishing to make
clear that human beings are morally responsible for their
actions, said, 'How is it that some are vessels of wrath, and
others of mercy? Of their own free choice (**apo pröaireseôs
oikeiâs**).' Augustine, however, who was obsessed with demonstrating the absolute sovereignty of God, believed that
human beings could not even begin to understand the work-
ings of God who showed mercy to them in accordance with
his inscrutable will. The difference in emphasis between
Chrysostom and Augustine was seized upon by later commentators, who used them in support of opposing views
regarding free will and predestination. Paul is simply making
the point that, as God has the right to choose who are to be his
children, the Jews cannot complain if God has chosen the
Gentiles to share in that honour; he is not concerned with the
wider implications of his argument.

'Which have been made fit for destruction', **katêrtismena eis
apôleian**, literally, 'equipped for destruction'. Paul does not
say 'whom God prepared for destruction'. Chrysostom sees
this as referring to Pharaoh, whom he describes as 'fully fitted,
but by himself and from his own resources'. Robinson
suggests 'they have become fit only for destruction'.

'These, indeed, are us, whom he called', **hous kai ekalesen
hêmâs**, literally, 'whom, indeed, he called us'. Paul is making
the point that not only Jews but also Gentiles are offered
salvation. This introduces a series of quotations from scripture
to prove that the calling of the Gentiles was part of God's plan.

25 As he also says in Hosea, 'I shall call a people who
are not mine "my people", and the unloved "beloved". 26 And it will happen in the place where it

was said to them, "You are not my people", that there they shall be called "the sons of the living God".' 27 But Isaiah cries out over Israel, 'If the number of the sons of Israel be as the sand of the sea, the remnant shall be saved. 28 For the Lord will bring his word to pass on the earth, fulfilling and curtailing.' 29 And as Isaiah has said before this, 'If the Lord of Hosts had not left us a seed, we would have become as Sodom, and likened to Gomorrah.'

[25] This quotation is a paraphrase of Hos. 2.23 (Sept. 2.25), 'And I shall have mercy on her who has not received mercy, and I shall say to the people who are not mine, "You are my people".'

[26] This is from Hos. 1.10 (Sept. 2.1), and apart from two minor variations is identical to the original.

'In the place' and 'there' are not to be understood as referring to a geographical location such as Palestine, but rather to the place previously occupied by Israel as the favoured people of God. In other words, it denotes the position and status held by his children.

[27, 28] Isa. 10.22, 23 (Sept.) is the original of this. Again there are a few variations, notably at the end of the quotation where the original has been much abbreviated. The AV version of v. 28, 'For he will finish the work, and cut it short *in righteousness*: *because a short work* will the Lord make upon the earth', is based on a manuscript tradition which included words from the original Sept. quotation omitted in the best texts.

'Word', **logon**, could be a legal 'sentence' (NEB) or a 'reckoning'.

'Fulfilling and curtailing' has several layers of meaning: the first term can mean 'fulfilling his word' or 'bringing things to a conclusion', and the second can mean 'cutting short the time' or 'reducing his people to a small remnant'.

[29] This is an exact quotation from Isa. 1.9.

'Has said before', **proeirêken**, i.e. earlier in the work, or 'has foretold'.

'Of Hosts', **sabaôth**.

For 'seed' see the notes on vv. 7, 8.

30 So what shall we say? That the Gentiles, who did not pursue righteousness, received righteousness, the righteousness [which comes] from faith, 31 but Israel, who pursued the Law of righteousness, did not catch up with the Law. 32 Why? Because [it was] not from faith but from works; they tripped on the stumbling stone, 33 as is written, 'Behold, I place in Sion a stumbling stone and a rock to trip over, and he who has faith in it shall not be put to shame.'

[30–33] Paul again brings the argument back to the distinction between the old and the new covenant, between justification from the works of the Law and the justification which comes through faith. God has rejected Israel not only because they did not succeed in keeping the Law but also because they have not accepted the new covenant which involves believing in Christ. The quotation is a conflation of Isa. 28.16 and 8.14.

'Catch up with', **ephthasen**, carries on the image of a person chasing after something and failing to catch it. The Jews chased after the Law but could not catch it, i.e. they failed to keep it, or, as Sanday and Headlam say, 'they did not attain it'.

'Stumbling stone', **lithon proskommatos**, and 'rock to trip over', **petrân skandalou**, are synonyms, clearly referring to

Christ. In Gal. 5.11 we have 'the stumbling block of the cross', **to skandalon tou staurou,** where it refers to the doctrine of atonement by the death of Christ. See my notes in *Reading through Galatians*.

'He who has faith', **ho pisteuôn,** literally, 'the one believing'. Remember that 'belief', 'trust' and 'faith' are all meanings of **pistis.**

The neuter 'in it', **ep'autôi,** is better grammar, since it refers to the stone, although we can translate it as 'in him', i.e. Christ.

Chapter 10

1 Brothers and sisters, the intention in my heart and my prayer to God is for them, that they should be saved. 2 For I bear witness for them that they have zeal for God, but it is not according to knowledge. 3 For, being ignorant of God's righteousness, and seeking to establish their own, they have not submitted themselves to God's righteousness. 4 For Christ is the end of the Law for every believer in regard to righteousness. 5 For Moses writes about the righteousness which comes from the Law, 'The man who has done them shall live by them.'

[1] 'Intention', **eudokiâ**, a word which covers a wide range of meanings such as 'consent', 'approval' and 'determination'. Sanday and Headlam reject the translation 'desire' (AV and NEB), but it can have this meaning.

[2] 'Zeal', **zêlon**, from which is derived the verb **zêloô** used by Paul in Gal. 4.17, 18 to refer to the enthusiastic way in which the Judaizers were trying to attract followers. The word 'zealot' comes from this word. See my notes on Gal. 4.17 in *Reading through Galatians*.

'Not according to knowledge' is explained by 'being ignorant of God's righteousness' in the next verse. They do not understand how the new covenant based on faith in Christ has enabled human beings to receive God's righteousness, i.e. justification. Paul frequently uses **epignôsis**, as he does here, instead of the common word for 'knowledge', **gnôsis**, when talking about the knowledge of God and his son or of an attribute of either, as I point out in the notes on 1.28. The word tends to mean 'recognition', particularly of a person.

[3] The 'righteousness' which they are 'seeking to establish' is justification by the works of the Law. God's 'righteousness' is justification which comes from faith in Christ.

[4] 'End', **telos**, here can have several meanings, such as 'termination', 'fulfilment', 'aim' and 'goal', despite Sanday and Headlam's assertion that it can only mean 'end' or 'termination'. Chrysostom says, 'What was the intention of the Law? To make man righteous. But it had not the power, since no one fulfilled it. This, then, was the **telos** of the Law, and it was to this that everything looked, and because of this that everything happened, the festivals, the commandments, the sacrifices and everything else.' Admittedly Christ put an end to the Law, but he also was its consummation; he was the one who brought the fulfilment of the Law and the one in whom the Law was meant to attain its purpose. See the notes on vv. 6–8. It is likely that in this verse the idea of putting an end to the role of the Law is uppermost in Paul's mind.

[5] Paul quotes from Lev. 18.5, a text he uses in Gal. 3.12, slightly altering the grammar to fit here. As in the Galatians passage, the point being made is that to be justified by the Law, and to receive eternal life, one has to carry out its comandments. In other words, actual performance is the condition imposed for justification.

6 But the righteousness [which comes] from faith says,

'Do not say in your heart, "Who will ascend to heaven?", that is, bring Christ down, 7 or, "Who will descend into the abyss?", that is, bring Christ up from the dead.' 8 Well, what does it say? 'The word is near you, in your mouth and in your heart,' that is, the word of faith which we preach, 9 namely, that if you confess with your mouth the Lord Jesus, and believe in your heart that God raised him from the dead, you shall be saved.

[6–8] This apparent quotation is a conflation which takes the start of Deut. 9.4, 'Do not say in your heart', continues with part of Deut. 30.12, 'Who will ascend to heaven?', and ends with a question probably suggested by Ps. 107.26 (Sept. 106.26), 'they descend into the depths', instead of the question found in the next verse of the Deuteronomy passage, 'who will cross over the sea?'. Paul then returns to Deut. 30.14 for the quotation in v. 8. The resulting composition, while modelled mainly on the passage in Deut. 30, says something subtly different. In vv. 10–13 Moses urges the Israelites to keep the *Torah*, and goes on to say that they will prosper if they listen to the voice of God and keep his commandments which are written in the book of the Law. There is no need to go up to heaven for the Law, or to cross over the sea for it.

Paul has substituted the new covenant of faith in Christ for the Mosaic Law, and is making the point that we do not have to go up to heaven or down to hell to look for Christ, since he is with us. All we have to do in order to be saved is to believe that he was raised from the dead and to confess that he is Lord. Note the substitution of the descent into the abyss for the crossing of the sea in the original. While the motif of the descent into the abyss is found in rabbinic tradition, Paul is using it here in reference to Christ's death and resurrection to affirm that he is no longer among the dead. Similarly, in speaking of going up to heaven, Paul is referring either to the incarnation (there is no need to ascend into heaven – he came down to earth for us) or to the ascension (although Christ ascended to heaven, he is still with us on earth). The latter interpretation is supported by Eph. 4.9, 10, where the descent into Hades is clearly linked with Christ's subsequent ascension, 'And what does this "he ascended" mean, if not that he also descended into the lower parts of the earth? The one who descended is the same one who ascended above all the heavens in order to fill all things.'

It is ironic that Paul has applied a text which originally referred to the Mosaic Law to the new Law of justification by faith. It might appear that he has deliberately altered the original sense by misquoting the text. As Sanday and Headlam say, 'In the OT the words are used by Moses of the Law: how can St Paul use them of the Gospel as against the Law?' Paul, however, would insist that he is not altering the original scripture but eliciting its hidden meaning, and he would argue that the real, spiritual message of the Deuteronomy passage has been brought out by his interpretation. In effect, he is taking Moses' words, which he has not quoted, i.e. 'if you listen to the voice of the Lord your God' and 'if you turn to the Lord your God with all your heart and with all your soul', as meaning 'if you believe in Christ'. After all, the spiritual Law has been made accessible and fulfilled by Christ. See my notes on 8.2.

'Word of faith' (v. 8), **rhêma tês pisteôs**, has been interpreted in various ways, but it is clear from the definition of it given in v. 9 that it is the *internal belief* in Christ expressed by such *external words* as 'Jesus is Lord'. Because it is described as the word 'which we preach' (or 'which we proclaim'), it is also the central message of the gospel. Paul very rarely uses the word **rhêma**, since the usual term for 'word' is **logos**, but, apart from the fact that it obviously

occurs here because it is the word used in the text which he is
quoting, **rhêma** has a special significance. As I point out in my
notes on Heb. 1.3 and 6.5 in *Reading through Hebrews*, it is
the word expressed in action. Hence to believe and to utter
the statement 'Jesus is Lord' is to cause certain things to
happen.

[9] 'Confess', **homologêsêis**, is a rare word in Paul's letters.
It can also mean 'agree', but the addition 'with your mouth'
shows that its use here is the same as we find in the Gospel
accounts (Matt. 10.32, Luke 12.8 and John 12.42), where
it denotes open acknowledgment of Christ. Note the way
Paul has picked up the words 'mouth' and 'heart' from the
Deuteronomy passage and given them a new interpretation.

10 For it is in the heart that one believes and is
justified, and with the mouth that one confesses and is
saved. 11 For the scripture says, 'Every one who
believes in him shall not be put to shame.' 12 For
there is no distinction between Jew and Greek, for [it
is] the same Lord over all, who is bountiful to all who
call upon him. 13 For 'Every one who calls upon the
name of the Lord shall be saved.'

[10] Paul develops his theme with the stylistic device of an
antithesis between the terms 'mouth' and 'heart', which is
balanced by an antithesis between 'justified' and 'saved'.
There is no theological significance in this. As Barrett observes
in his comment on the previous verse, 'No distinction is to be
drawn between the confession and the faith; the confession is
believed and the faith confessed.'

'And is justified', literally, 'for righteousness', **eis dikaiosynên**; similarly, 'and is saved', 'for salvation', **eis sôtêriân**.

[11] This is a repetition of the quotation used in 9.33, but with the addition of 'every one'.

[12] For the word 'distinction', see my notes on 3.22.

'Greek', as in 1.16, is a synonym for Gentile.

'Who is bountiful', **ploutôn**, literally, 'being rich'. The 'wealth' of God is not just what he owns but what he gives away, as we can see in 2.4; Col. 1.27; Eph. 1.7, 8; 1.18; 2.7; and many other places in the NT. See my notes on Col. 1.27 in *Reading through Colossians and Ephesians*.

[13] This quotation comes from Joel 2.32 (Sept. 3.5). It appears that 'the Lord' here is Christ and that Paul is referring back to v. 9 and the confession that Jesus is Lord. The significance of attaching to Christ an epithet, which in the original OT passage refers to God, is inescapable; as Paul sees it, Christ shares his Father's divinity.

14 How, then, are they to call on him whom they did not believe, how are they to believe on him whom they have not heard, and how are they to hear unless someone announces the news? 15 And how are they to announce the news unless they are sent? As it is written, 'How beautiful are the feet of those who tell the good news!' 16 But not everyone accepted the good news. For Isaiah says, 'Lord, who has believed our report?' 17 So belief comes from hearing, and hearing through the word of Christ.

[14] This passage has been interpreted by some commentators either as Paul's justification for preaching the gospel to the Gentiles or as proof for the necessity of an authorized ministry, but neither interpretation is relevant. Paul has just said that God's salvation is readily available to anyone who

calls upon the name of the Lord. This verse introduces a series of possible objections from his opponents, or rather excuses, on the grounds that the Jews have not heard the gospel which tells them about this way of salvation, and therefore cannot be blamed for not accepting it. They would argue that they cannot be expected to believe in someone whom they had not personally heard and about whom they had heard nothing from any one else, in other words, either directly or indirectly. But as Chrysostom rightly points out, God has done everything possible by his prophets and apostles to inform the Jews about his son and the salvation which he brought: 'if they did not believe, it was entirely their own fault.'

'Whom they have not heard' fits the grammar and the argument better than the AV '*of* whom they have not heard' or the NEB 'one they had never heard *of*'.

'Unless someone announces the news', **chôris kêryssontos**, literally, 'apart from an announcer'.

[15] The objection implied here is that no prophet was appointed by God to proclaim the gospel of Christ. Paul counters this with a quotation from Isa. 52.7, which, unusually, is closer to the Hebrew than the Septuagint. Some manuscripts add the clause 'of those telling the good news of peace', probably to make it conform more closely to the Sept. version. The choice of this quotation, which occurs in a passage which Jews regarded as Messianic, is intended to show that God did send prophets to proclaim the gospel. It is also worth noting that the next chapter of Isaiah refers to the rejection of the Messiah.

'Beautiful', **hôraioi**, not 'welcome' (NEB). It is true that it comes from **hôrâ**, 'time' or 'season', and in classical Greek usually means 'seasonable' or 'ripe', but, as in modern Greek, in the NT it only means 'beautiful': for example, 'the Beautiful Gate' of the Temple is **hê hôraiâ pylê**.

[16] Sanday and Headlam regard this as another objection, 'Yet, in spite of the fact that this message was sent, all did not obey the Gospel'. It is better to treat it as a comment by Paul, who is making the point that the good news *was* announced, even if it was not accepted by everybody. The quotation is from Isa. 53.1.

'Accepted', **hypêkousan**, literally, 'obeyed'.

'Report', **akoêi**, in Heb. 4.2 is associated with **logos**, and the phrase **logos akoês**, as I point out in my notes on that verse, is almost a synonym for 'the gospel'. **Akoê** usually means 'hearing', as in the next verse, but here means 'the thing one hears'.

[17] Paul is dismissing the excuses of his opponents: they *have* heard, so they *can* believe. Furthermore, they have heard the gospel of Christ, i.e. 'the word of Christ', **rhêmatos Christou**, which recalls the **rhêma tês pisteôs** of v .8. See the notes on that verse.

18 But I say, surely they had not heard? On the contrary, 'Their sound went out into every land, and their words to the limits of the inhabited world.' 19 But I say, surely Israel did not know? Moses was the the first to say, 'I shall provoke you to jealousy over a [nation that is] no nation; I shall anger you over a nation without understanding.' 20 Isaiah is bold and says, 'I was found among those who were not seeking me; I was made manifest to those who were not inquiring of me.' 21 But to Israel he says, 'All day I stretched out my hands to a disobedient and contrary people.'

[18] 'But I say', which is repeated in the next verse, is

definitely an objection put into the mouth of an opponent, which Paul counters with an exact quotation from Ps. 19.4 (Sept. 18.5). The use of the first person here to express the thoughts of an opponent recalls its use in 7.14–24, and is strong evidence against interpreting that famous outburst as genuinely autobiographical. See the notes on that passage.

'On the contrary', **menounge**, as in 9.20, is used to introduce a statement correcting something previously said.

[19] This quotation is from Deut. 32.21, substituting 'you' for 'them'. The point the objector seems to be making is that the Jews did not know that they would lose the special favour of God. Paul answers with a quotation which proves that even a prophet as early as Moses had warned them that God would abandon them in favour of the Gentiles.

[20] This comes from Isa. 65.1, with the clause order inverted. It reinforces the previous reference to God turning to the Gentiles.

[21] This continues the previous quotation (Isa. 65.2) with a slight variation in word order. This quotation makes the point that God had rejected the Jews only after he had appealed in vain for them to come back to him.

Chapter 11

1 I say then, surely God has not rejected his people?
Certainly not. For I also am an Israelite, of the seed of
Abraham, of the tribe of Benjamin. 2 God has not
rejected his people whom he knew beforehand. Or do
you not know what the scripture says in [the story of]
Elijah, how he appeals to God regarding Israel, 3
'Lord, they have killed your prophets, dug up your
altars, and I alone am left and they are seeking my
life'? 4 But what does the divine response say to him?
'I have left for myself seven thousand men, who have
not bowed the knee to Baal.' 5 So, in the same way, at
the present time also a remnant has been created,
selected by grace, 6 and if by grace, it can no longer be
as a result of works, [otherwise] grace is no longer
grace.

[1] 'I say', as previously, is Paul's opponent speaking. Paul's
reply is usually interpreted as an affirmation that, because he
himself, a Jew, had not been rejected, God had not rejected
the Jews. It is also possible to take it as a statement which
proves that Paul was not biased against the Jews, since he was
one himself.

'Rejected', **apôsato**, literally, 'pushed away', a word rarely
found in the NT. Paul is deliberately recalling, as Sanday and

Headlam point out, the promise of I Sam. 12.22 and Ps. 94.14 (Sept. 93), 'the Lord *will not reject* (**apôsetai**) his people'.

[2] 'Knew beforehand', **pröegnô**, is a complex term, with at least four meanings:

1. 'knew and chose beforehand', i.e. 'predetermined';
2. 'knew about beforehand', i.e. 'had foreknowledge of';
3. 'knew from a previous time', i.e. 'was acquainted with from way back';
4. 'knew before he knew any other people', i.e. 'preferred'.

In 8.29 this verb clearly suggests the idea of predetermination, 'those whom he *knew beforehand* (**pröegnô**) he also *ordained beforehand* (**pröôrisen**) should share the form of his son's likeness'. But in Acts 26.5, in a passage where Paul is telling Agrippa about his former life as a Pharisee, he goes on to speak of the Jews '*who knew me before* (**progînôskontes me**) from the beginning'. Here we clearly find the verb used in the third sense. All of these meanings may co-exist here.

'Appeals', **entyngchanei**, i.e. 'makes an accusation', not 'pleads for' or 'intercedes for' as in 8.27, 34.

[3] This is a quotation from I Kings (Sept. III Kings – because I and II Sam. are called I and II Kings in the Septuagint) 19.10, or 19.14, where it is repeated, with omissions and several variations in word order and vocabulary.

[4] The quotation is from v. 18 of the same chapter of I Kings, with several variations which indicate that Paul may be quoting from the original Hebrew or another translation.

'Divine response', **chrêmatismos**, Vulg. *responsum divinum*, AV 'answer of God'. The NEB 1961 edition translated this word as 'oracle' but in the second edition changed it to 'divine voice'. See my note on 3.2 for the reason why 'oracle' is incorrect.

'Baal' means 'Lord' and was originally used to address the God of Israel. Since it was also used to address the god of the Phoenicians, it was discontinued as an epithet for the Jewish God (see Hos. 2.16), in order to avoid confusion. In the Septuagint the feminine word **aischûnê**, 'shame', for the Hebrew *bosheth*, i.e. 'abomination', was sometimes substituted for 'Baal', as in v. 25 of the previous chapter of the same book of Kings, and it seems also to have been the custom when reciting the Greek version of scripture to use the word **aischûnê** when the abominable name 'Baal' occurred in the text. This is why the feminine definite article **têi**, not the masculine **tôi**, is found here attached to 'Baal'.

[5] Just as in the days of Elijah, God has preserved a faithful remnant of true Israelites, namely, the Jews who have accepted Jesus as Lord. The disobedient majority and the faithful minority is the main theme of Stephen's speech in Acts 7 which led to his martyrdom.

'Remnant', **leimma**, is found nowhere else in the NT.

'Selected by grace', **kat'eklogên charitos**, literally, 'according to a selection of grace'.

[6] Paul is insisting that God decides who his chosen people will be; it is not a privilege earned by fulfilling certain obligations, but a free gift. Although Paul does not define 'works', it is highly probable that he is referring to the 'works of the Law'.

7 What then? Israel has not obtained what it has been seeking, but the selection has; the rest were hardened. 8 As it is written, 'God gave them a spirit of stupefaction, eyes so that they may not see and ears that they may not hear, up to the present day.' 9 And David says, 'Let their table be as a snare and a trap, as a stumbling block and a retribution to them; 10 let their eyes be darkened

so that they cannot see, and bend down their backs for ever.' 11 So I say, surely they have not stumbled so they should fall? God forbid! No, [it was in order that] salvation [might come] to the Gentiles through their failing, [and] in order to cause them to be jealous. 12 And if their failing is the enrichment of the world, and their loss the enrichment of the Gentiles, how much more [an enrichment will be] their fulfilment?

[7] The meaning of this abbreviated verse is that some Jews, i.e. 'the selection', **hê eklogê**, have been granted salvation, but 'the rest', **hoi loipoi**, while ostensibly seeking salvation and righteousness, i.e. 'justification', have rejected the justification which comes through faith, and consequently have been rejected by God.

'Were hardened', **epôrôthêsan**, not 'were blinded' (AV) or 'were made blind' (NEB). This verb is used in medicine to describe the formation of a callus. In the NT it is a metaphor for the formation of an insensitive layer over the heart. The difference between making blind and hardening is made clear in John 12.40, 'He has *blinded* (**tetyphlôken**) their eyes and *hardened* (**epôrôsen**) their hearts'. See my note on Eph. 4.18 in *Reading through Colossians and Ephesians*.

[8] The quotation seems to be a conflation of Deut. 29.4 (Sept. 29.3), Isa. 29.10 and Isa. 6.9, 10.

'Stupefaction', **katanyxeôs**, from a verb meaning 'to stab', hence 'to stun'.

[9, 10] 'David says', i.e. in Psalm 69.22, 23 (Sept. 68.23, 24), with variations in the first verse. The image suggested is a scene where people are caught unawares by their enemies while enjoying a feast. Alternatively, the table represents the offerings made according to the Mosaic Law.

'Trap', **thêrân**, literally 'hunting' or 'prey', has been added by Paul to the original, probably from Ps. 35.8 (Sept. 34.8), where it is found in association with the word for 'snare', **pagis**.

[11] 'So I say' introduces another remark from an imaginary objector who cannot believe that Israel will be cast off for ever, 'They might have stumbled, but surely this does not mean they have fallen never to get up again?' Paul immediately counters this with the assurance that, firstly, God has used their failure, i.e. the rejection of the gospel of Christ, as an opportunity to extend salvation to the Gentiles, and, secondly, God wishes, by demonstrating the blessings which the Gentiles are receiving, to provoke the Jews to give up their stubbornness and imitate the Gentiles.

'Failing', **paraptômati**, which I have previously translated as 'sin' or 'transgression'. See my notes on Eph. 2.1 in *Reading through Colossians and Ephesians*.

[12] 'Enrichment', **ploutos**, literally, 'wealth'.

'Failing' and 'loss', **hêttêma**, seem to be contrasted with 'fulfilment', **plêrôma**. Commentators differ in their interpretations, but if **plêrôma** is taken in its usual NT sense, as 'fullness', 'fulfilment' or 'perfection', Paul is saying that if even the failure of the Jews to accept the gospel has been a source of blessings to the rest of the world, their perfection, i.e. their accepting the gospel and the fulfilling of their destiny as God's chosen people, will be even more the enrichment of all. Compare NEB 'But if their offence means the enrichment of the world, and if their falling-off means the enrichment of the Gentiles, how much more their coming to full strength!' Some take Paul to be contrasting the present state of the Jews, so few of them accepting the gospel, with the prospect of them all, i.e. the full complement, accepting it, but neither 'failing' nor 'loss' can stand for 'the present faithful remnant', even though **plêrôma** can denote a 'full complement' in classical literature. More seriously, it misses the point: Paul is contrasting the enrichment of the world by the contribution made by the Jews *up to the present time* with its potential enrichment *in the future*, not the small size of the faithful remnant with the large numbers of the full complement. This point is made clearer in v. 15. See my notes on **plêrôma** in Col. 1.19; 2.9; Eph. 1.23; 3.19.

13 I am speaking to you Gentiles, [and I am telling you that] I actually extol my ministry as an apostle of the Gentiles, 14 with the hope that I might make my flesh [and blood] jealous, and save some of them. 15 For if their rejection [has proved to be] the reconciliation of the world, what [will] their acceptance [be], if not life from death? 16 If the first piece [of dough] is holy, so is the rest of the lump; and if the root is holy, so are the branches. 17 But if some of the branches were cut away, and you, the wild olive, were grafted in among them and shared the olive's root and fertility, 18 do not boast over the branches; if you do, [remember] it is not you who bear the root, but the root which bears you.

[13, 14] The language of these verses is not easy to follow, and the irony is missed in most translations. One should visualize Paul turning to the Gentiles and saying, like an actor delivering an aside on the stage, 'Don't tell your Jewish friends, but I always make a great deal of my special relationship with you so that some of them at least may become jealous and want to share your faith.' Sanday and Headlam take the fact that Paul is addressing the Gentiles here as due to his remembering that the majority of his audience were Gentiles. This is reading far too much into an aside. We cannot possibly prove that the Gentiles were the majority from such evidence.

'Actually', **men oun**, rather like **menounge**, introducing a new idea which corrects or modifies some previous statement.

'Extol', **doxazô**, i.e. 'glorify'.

[15] 'Reconciliation', **katallagê**; see note on 5.10 regarding the verb 'to reconcile'.

'From death', literally, 'from the dead'. The idea seems to be that the conversion of the whole nation of Israel will herald the final resurrection of the dead. Others interpret this merely as a figure of speech, i.e. the conversion of Israel will be a sort of resurrection of the dead, but Paul is most probably comparing the *present* state, where the world is already being reconciled to God because the rejection by the Jews of the gospel has led to the extension of salvation to the Gentiles, with the *future* event of the final day of resurrection, when all of Israel will accept the rule of Christ.

[16] The thinking behind the first metaphor can be illustrated from Num. 15.19, 20 (AV), 'Then it shall be, that, when ye eat of the bread of the land, ye shall offer up an heave offering unto the Lord. Ye shall offer up a cake of the first of your dough for an heave offering.' The second metaphor of the olive tree, which represents Israel, is derived from such passages as Jer. 11.16 (AV), 'The Lord called thy name, A green olive tree, fair, and of goodly fruit.' Chrysostom points out that the 'first piece' and the 'root' represent the holy patriarchs, such as Abraham, Isaac and Jacob, and the prophets, 'all the distinguished people of the Old Testament'. The 'rest of the lump' and the 'branches' are the individual believers who depend upon them. By reminding the Gentiles of the debt which both Gentile and Jewish Christians owe to the holy patriarchs and prophets, and of the fact that they belong to the same lump (or, following the second metaphor, are only fellow branches dependent on the same stock), Paul

warns them not to be proud, and at the same time reassures his Jewish listeners.

'First piece', **aparchê**; see note on 8.23.

[17, 18] The Gentiles are reminded that they were grafted on to the stock of the olive tree, and are supported by it; they do not support it. We need not pay too much attention to the agricultural experts who question Paul's grasp of farming techniques and point out that one normally uses grafts from the cultivated olive. Paul is notoriously careless about detail when using metaphors. We can take it that he knew that one does not normally graft wild olive on to the cultivated variety. He admits as much in v. 24.

'Shared', literally, 'became *a joint-sharer*' (**syngkoinônos**), i.e. along with the Jewish Christians.

'Fertility', **pîotêtos**, literally, 'fatness'.

19 You will say then, 'The branches were cut away so that I might be grafted in.' 20 Fine, they were cut away due to their unfaithfulness, while you are fixed there due to your faith. But beware and do not think too highly of yourself. 21 For if God did not spare the natural branches, perhaps he may not spare you either. 22 So note the kindness and the severity of God, severity to those who have fallen, but kindness to you, provided you stay within his kindness, otherwise you too will be cut out. 23 They also will be grafted in, if they do not remain in [a state of] unfaithfulness, since God is capable of grafting them in again. 24 For if you were cut out of your natural wild olive and, against nature, grafted into a culti-vated olive, how much more [easily] will these natural [branches] be grafted into their own olive?

[19, 20] 'You' is the Gentile Christian who might argue that God has deliberately rejected the Jews in order to replace them with the Gentiles. Paul agrees that the Jews were rejected, but only because of their unfaithfulness. Faith and obedience is the condition for admission to and for remaining in the new covenant, and the Gentiles are reminded that their continued acceptance depends on this.

'Beware', **phobou**, literally, 'be afraid'.

'Do not think too highly of yourself', **mê hypsêla phronei**, literally, 'do not think high things'. **Hypsêlos**, in addition to the morally neutral 'high', can also have the negative meaning 'boastful' and the positive 'sublime'.

[21] 'The natural branches', **tôn kata physin kladôn**, literally, 'the branches according to nature', here represent the Jews who have not accepted Christ. See note on 2.14.

'Perhaps', **mê pôs**, literally, 'lest in some way', is missing in several good manuscripts, but it is well attested and is represented by the Vulg. *ne forte*. The expression is found with verbs of fearing, and, although the verb of fearing has been omitted, that is most probably the construction here, i.e. '*beware* lest in some way . . .', hence the AV 'take heed . . .'. It is likely that the missing verb is **phobou**, 'beware', which is in the previous verse.

[22] 'Kindness', **chrêstotêta**; see note on 2.4.

'Severity', **apotomiân**, occurs only here in the NT. It is derived from the adjective **apotomos**, 'sheer' or 'cut off', which when applied to people can mean 'brusque' or 'severe'. It is also used as a technical word to denote a fight to the death in gladiatorial contests.

'Those who have fallen' are the Jews who reject Christ. This recalls the reference in v. 11.

'Otherwise', as in the AV and NEB, is substituted for the literal 'since', **epei**.

[23] This softens the reference in the previous verse to God's severity towards the Jews who do not accept Christ. If they repent, they also will be saved.

[24] The 'natural wild olive' stands for the former status of the Gentile Christians. Their incorporation into the body of the church is 'against nature' in the sense that they had previously been outside the community of Israel. Accordingly, the 'natural branches', being Jews, would be returning to their 'natural' community. As Sanday and Headlam demonstrate from rabbinic literature, Jewish theologians taught that the merits of the holy patriarchs would protect the Jews from retribution on the Day of Judgment. Paul would obviously not support such a view; they can only be saved by faith. Nevertheless, it is clear from Paul's comment in v. 28, 'they are loved because of their forefathers', that the faith of the patriarchs, and the fact that they were the original chosen nation, did in some way keep the Jews as a whole in a special relationship with God.

25 For I want you, brothers and sisters, not to be ignorant of this secret, so that you may not be wise in your own eyes, that hardness has come upon part of Israel, until such a time as the fullness of the Gentiles enters in. 26 And in this way shall all of Israel be saved; as it is written, 'There shall come from Sion a deliverer; he will turn aside impieties from Jacob. 27 And this shall be their covenant from me, when I take away their sins.' 28 In regard to the gospel, they are enemies because of you, but in regard to the election, they are loved because of their forefathers. 29 For the gifts and the calling of God are not revoked.

[25] The 'secret', **mystêrion**, as I explain in the notes on Col. 1.26 in *Reading through Colossians and Ephesians*, is God's hidden purpose which has now been revealed with the coming of Christ.

'Wise in your own eyes', **par'heautois phronimoi**, literally, 'wise in one's own presence'. The NEB 'complacent about your own discernment' is an obscure expression. Sanday and Headlam interpret this phrase as 'imagining that it is in any way through your own merit that you have accepted what others have refused', but Paul is simply warning the Gentile Christians not to think that they know everything; God's plans are beyond their comprehension.

'Hardness', **pôrôsis**; see note on v. 7.

'Part of Israel', literally, 'Israel in part'.

'Fullness', **plêrôma**, is both the perfection of the converted Gentiles and the completed tally of converts, i.e. 'the full complement'. One need not take it as referring to some historical point of time, when a certain number of Gentiles has been counted past the post, after which event the conversion of the Jews will follow, but rather as the final culmination when all things reach their goal in the second coming of Christ. See the notes on v. 12.

'Enters in', i.e. into the kingdom. This verb is frequently followed in the Gospels by such phrases as 'the kingdom of heaven' or 'life'.

[26, 27] The quotation starts with Isa. 59.20, with a minor variation, but switches in v. 27 to Isaiah 27.9 for the clause 'when I take away their sins'. Isa. 27.9 in full reads, 'Because of this the lawlessness of Jacob shall be taken away, and this is *his blessing*, when I take away *his* sin.' The variation in the latter quotation is probably because it is not taken from the Septuagint.

'All of Israel' is 'Israel as a whole', i.e. the Jews as a nation, not every individual Israelite. The rabbis taught that all of

Israel had a share in the world to come, but defined 'all of Israel' in such a way that it certainly excluded the wicked, such as magicians, heretics, the licentious, etc., as Barrett points out. There is no warrant for taking 'Israel' here as the spiritual Israel, i.e. the body of Christian believers; Paul is clearly speaking of the Jewish nation.

[28] This verse sums up the argument of the previous section, i.e. that the Jews may have rejected the gospel, but they are still in a special relationship with God.

'Enemies because of you', i.e. treated as hostile by God so that you Gentiles might be saved. The falling away of the Jews enabled the gospel to be extended to the rest of the world.

'In regard to the election', **kata tên eklogên**, i.e. inasmuch as they are God's chosen people. As Sanday and Headlam note, this is not a reference to the select remnant of vv. 5 and 7.

[29] This echoes the thought of Heb. 6.17, 18, 'In this matter God, wishing to make absolutely clear to the heirs of the promise the unalterable nature of his will, intervened with an oath, so that through two unalterable matters, where God could not lie, we who have fled to him for refuge should have a firm encouragement . . .' God is faithful and keeps his word, even though human beings are faithless.

'Not revoked', **ametamelêta**, literally, 'not to be repented of'. The use of the word 'gifts', **charismata**, underlines the point Paul is making, that God's mercy and goodness towards mankind and his invitation, i.e. 'calling', **klêsis**, to enter the kingdom is not a reward for good deeds but a manifestation of grace, i.e. **charis**. He does not change his mind, even though we might do so.

30 For, as you once were disobedient to God, but have now received mercy through their disobedience,

31 so have they, too, now disobeyed through the
mercy shown to you, in order that they, too, may now
receive mercy. 32 For God has confined all to
disobedience, so that he may show mercy to all. 33
O the depths of God's riches, wisdom and knowledge!
How inscrutable are his judgments and unfathomable
his ways! 34 For who has known the mind of the
Lord, or who has been his counsellor? 35 Who has
given [anything] first to him to be given it in return?
36 For all things [come] from him and through him
and end in him. Glory be to him for ever, amen.

[30–32] Paul is still addressing the Gentiles. The thought here
is complex, and the interpretation hinges on the precise
meaning of the two datives, **apeitheiâi** and **elëei,** in the phrases
'through their disobedience' and 'through the mercy shown to
you' respectively. The NEB takes them as having simply a
temporal sense, 'in the time of their disobedience' and 'when
you receive mercy', but there is clearly a causal connection
between the Gentiles receiving mercy and the rejection of the
gospel by the Jews. Barrett suggests 'corresponding to . . .' as
a way of expressing the connection, and points out that 'more
is involved than mere instrumentality and temporality'.

As we have noted before, Paul's use of antithesis and his
abbreviated style make his thought hard to follow. What he
seems to be saying is something like this: 'You Gentiles were
once disobedient, being outside the covenant of Israel. But
God turned to you because of the faithlessness of the Jews,
and as a result of their disobedience, you were allowed to
share this new covenant in their place. Their disobedience
enabled mercy to be shown to you. They have continued to
reject God and his gospel, and do not accept that Gentiles can
share in the promises originally made to Abraham, but the

same mercy which was shown to disobedient Gentiles can also be extended to disobedient Jews.' The conclusion is spelled out in verse 32: 'Everyone has had to go through a stage of disobedience in order to be shown mercy.' The problem here is typical: Paul is trying to say too much at once.

'Confined', **synekleisen**, literally, 'enclosed together', but with the meaning of 'gave over to so that they could not escape'. This is an idiom found in the Septuagint, e.g. Ps. 78.62 (Sept. 77), '*he gave* his people *over* (**synekleisen**) to the sword'.

[33] 'Depths of riches', **bathos ploutou**, i.e. the bottomless treasury of good things which God pours out. Compare 9.23, 'the treasures of his glory', **ton plouton tês doxês autou,** and see note on 10.12.

'Unfathomable', **anexichniastoi,** occurs in only one other place in the NT, Eph. 3.8, 'the unfathomable treasures of Christ'.

[34] This comes from Isa. 40.13, with slight variations.

[35] This clearly comes from Job 41.11, but not from the Septuagint, although v. 3 of that version seems vaguely to correspond to it. Sanday and Headlam note that it is closer to the Hebrew, and that the only other quotation in Paul which varies considerably from the Septuagint is also taken from the book of Job.

'To be given it in return', literally, 'and it will be given back to him'.

[36] The NEB paraphrases the first part of this verse with 'Source, Guide, and Goal of all that is'.

Chapter 12

1 So I beseech you, brothers and sisters, by the mercy of God, to present your bodies as a living, holy sacrifice, well-pleasing to God, as your spiritual worship, 2 and do not assume the fashion of this world, but transform yourselves by the renewal of your minds so that you can discern the will of God, what is good, well-pleasing [to him] and perfect. 3 For I am telling every one of you, through the grace given to me, not to think more highly [of himself] than he should, but to think sensible thoughts, according to the measure of faith which God has given each one [of you]. 4 For just as we have many members in one body, but all the members do not have the same function, 5 so we, the many, are one body in Christ, and each one of us members of one another.

[1] Many commentators treat this and the succeeding chapters as totally separate from the preceding ones. But, as Barrett says, it is a serious mistake to treat the two parts of the letter as distinct from each other. In this verse Paul links the previous sections on the relevance of the Mosaic Law with the new subject of the Christian way of life. The subtle connection which he makes between the fleshly sacrifices of the old covenant and the spiritual sacrifices of the new can

easily be missed. Firstly, 'sacrifice', **thysiân**, occurs fifteen times in the letter to the Hebrews and always in the context of the sacrifices carried out by the levitical high priest. Secondly, the word 'holy', **hagiân**, is one of the epithets used in the Septuagint to describe the sacrificial animals required by the Law, the other being 'blameless', **amômos**, which is found linked with 'holy' in Col. 1.22, 'to present you as holy, blameless and free from reproach'. See my notes on that passage in *Reading through Colossians and Ephesians*. Finally, the use of the term 'living' is clearly meant to contrast with the animals which were killed in the Mosaic sacrifice.

'Mercy' is actually 'mercies', **oiktirmôn**, following the use of the plural in the Septuagint.

'As your spiritual worship', **tên logikên latreiân hûmôn**, which Chrysostom glosses as 'spiritual ministry, a life which is lived in accordance with Christ'. Clearly there is also an implied contrast with the 'fleshly' rites of the Mosaic Law, which Chrysostom hints at by comparing the old sacrifice of brute beasts, 'cattle *without reason* (**aloga**)', with the new self-offering of rational human beings. The AV 'which is your reasonable service', which recalls the Vulg. *rationabile obsequium vestrum*, unfortunately means nowadays 'the service which one might reasonably expect of you'. Strictly speaking, **logikos**, which derives from **logos**, means 'rational', but Paul is using the word in a different sense. The NEB translates the phrase as 'the worship offered by mind and heart', giving it an emotional bias which is completely lacking in the original, although it has in a footnote the alternative translation, 'for such is the worship which you, as rational creatures, should offer'.

[2] 'Do not assume the fashion of this world', **mê syschêmatizesthe tôi aiôni toutôi**, literally, 'do not be modelled together with this age'.

'Transform yourselves', **metamorphousthe**, a word used to

describe the transfiguration of Jesus in the Gospel accounts (Matt. 17.2 and Mark 9.2). Chrysostom contrasts the unstable and temporary nature of the noun **schêma**, 'fashion', with the more stable and permanent reality of **morphê**, 'form'. The AV 'be not *conformed* to this world: but be ye *transformed*' is another example of the influence of the Vulgate, which here has *nolite conformari huic saeculo, sed transformamini*. This word play, however, is not in the original, since the Greek verbs do not come from a common root.

'The renewal of your minds' is a part of the 'transforma-tion' made possible by the gift of the Holy Spirit. The only other use in the NT of the word **anakainôsis**, 'renewal', is found in Titus 3.5: 'He saved us, not as a result of the works of righteousness which we carried out, but according to his mercy through the washing of regeneration and *renewal* by the Holy Spirit.'

'Discern', **dokimazein**; see notes on 1.28 and 2.18.

[3] There is a heavy play on words here which it is impossible to reproduce in translation. 'To think more highly', **hyper-phronein**, is echoed by 'to think', **phronein** (which occurs twice in the original) and **sôphronein**, 'to be prudent' (translated here as 'think sensible thoughts'). 'To think more highly' of oneself is not a reference to giving oneself airs or behaving generally in an arrogant fashion, but must be taken in the context of the following verses. Paul is referring to the functions and offices of the individual members of the church and reminding his audience that each Christian has a special place in that body and that they are all dependent on each other. 'The measure of faith' is, as Sanday and Headlam point out, a reference to the gifts which are given to each member 'with or as the result of his faith'.

There is no need to interpret this passage as dealing solely with the problems caused by the so-called 'charismatics'. *All* gifts of the Holy Spirit are 'charismatic', as the word **charisma-**

ta, which is used in v. 6, means simply 'free gifts', and, since they are given by 'the Spirit', **to pneuma,** they are *all* 'pneumatic'. The whole life of the church is 'charismatic', according to Barrett, and, as Käsemann says, every Christian is a charismatic. Paul is concerned here with the efficient and harmonious functioning of the whole community, not a particular section of it, and in warning its members that they should cooperate and not act as though their particular gifts separated them from the rest, there is no evidence that he is thinking exclusively of the more exuberant manifestations of the Spirit.

[4, 5] These verses clearly foreshadow the doctrine of the church as the body of Christ, which is fully developed in later works such as Colossians and Ephesians. The image of the community as a body is also found in classical literature.

6 As we have gifts which differ according to the grace given to us [let us use them], if prophecy, [let us prophesy] according to the proportion of faith, 7 if service, [do it] with service, the teacher by teaching, 8 the counsellor by counsel, the one who gives to others with simplicity, the office holder with zeal and the one who performs acts of mercy with gladness. 9 [Let] your love [be] without pretence, hating evil and clinging to the good, 10 in love of the brotherhood, tender and affectionate to one another, treating the other person as more important than oneself, 11 not hesitant in zeal, [but] fervent in spirit, serving the Lord, 12 rejoicing in hope, patient in suffering, persevering in prayer, 13 contributing to the needs of the saints, cultivating hospitality.

The details of this passage, and, indeed, of the rest of the chapter, are not easy to follow, since it is very condensed and the grammatical structure is irregular. For instance, there is no main verb in the long sentence of vv. 6–8. Hence one could treat it as a statement, although it makes better sense to treat it as an exhortation. The general meaning, however, is plain.

[6] 'According to the proportion of faith', **kata tên analogiân tês pisteôs**, is not easy to understand, but it must be related to the phrase 'according to the measure of faith' in v. 3. **Analogiâ** is used to denote mathematical proportion or ratio, but it is also connected with the verb **analogizomai**, 'calculate', 'sum up', and so may mean here the gifts which have been put down to the account of the individual believer. It has been suggested that it refers to the account which the individual takes of his own faith, but this is most unlikely. The general interpretation is that a person with the gift of prophecy should exercise this gift in proportion to the faith that he has. He should not try to go beyond his capabilities.

[7] Note that Paul starts his list with abstract nouns, i.e. 'prophecy', and 'service', but changes to participles, **ho didaskôn**, i.e. 'the one teaching', and **ho parakalôn**, 'the one counselling'.

'Service', **diâkoniân**, is a term used in particular to refer to the administration of alms and the material support of those in the Christian community who needed it. The term 'deacon' quickly emerged as the name of a person performing a particular ministry in the church.

[8] 'Counsellor', **parakalôn**, from a verb which can mean 'comfort', 'console', 'encourage' and 'support'. The term **paraklêtos**, which was applied by John to the Holy Spirit, and which is traditionally translated as 'comforter', is used elsewhere to denote a legal adviser or advocate in court. The NEB translation, 'one who has the gift of stirring speech', is too narrow.

'The one who gives to others', **ho metadidous**, literally, 'the one who gives a share', could also be translated as 'the one who contributes to charitable causes'.

'Simplicity', **haplotêti**, is a word which carries a wide range of meanings. The core meaning is 'singleness', hence 'plainness' or 'frankness', but it also was used to denote 'openhandedness', i.e. 'generosity'. Perhaps here it means 'with no ulterior motives'.

'The office holder', **ho proïstamenos**, i.e. 'the leader'.

[9] 'Clinging to', **kollômenoi**, literally, 'being glued to'.

[10] 'Love of the brotherhood', **philadelphiâi**, is not a common word in Paul's letters, occurring only here and in I Thess. 4.9. It denotes the love within a family. Similarly, the term 'tender and affectionate', **philostorgoi**, is nearly always found in the context of the family. The family here, of course, is the Christian community.

'Treating the other person as more important than oneself', **têi tîmêi allêlous proêgoumenoi**, i.e. 'accounting one another ahead in honour'. The verb **proêgoumai** normally means 'go ahead and lead', hence some commentators take it as meaning here 'taking the lead in showing honour' or 'taking the lead in honourable actions'. This is the sense suggested by the Vulg. *honore praevenientes*. Such an interpretation, however, is dubious, and the obvious meaning, if we take the verb in its normal sense, ought to be 'taking the lead in honour *over* others', which is the very opposite to the one intended. **Proêgoumai** is a compound of **hêgoumai**, which can mean either 'I lead' or 'I think', and it has been suggested that Paul is using this verb to mean 'I think [others] superior', since he has a similar expression in Phil. 2.3, '*thinking* (**hêgoumenoi**) one another *superior* (**hyperechontas**) to oneself'. As **proêgoumai** does not occur elsewhere in the NT, we cannot be sure of the precise meaning here, although the general sense is clear.

[11] 'Spirit' here is most probably 'the Holy Spirit'.

'Serving the _Lord_', **kûriôi**, is the most likely reading, although some manuscripts have 'serving the _time_', **kairôi**, which creates a phrase very like one used in 13.11, 'knowing the time'. Jerome took **kûriôi** as the correct reading here. He was aware of the alternative **kairôi**, since he specifically rejects it in a private letter to Marcella (_Letter_ 27).

[12] 'Rejoicing in hope', **têi elpidi chairontes**; the NEB 'let hope keep you joyful' distorts the meaning. Paul is saying that Christians should rejoice because of their expectation of eternal life, not that they should be hopeful in order to be joyful.

[13] 'Needs', **chreiais**, Vulg. _necessitatibus_, is the reading of the best manuscripts. A few have **mneiais**, 'remembrances', which would refer to memorials of the dead, and its occurrence here probably reflects, as Käsemann claims, 'the practice of intercession for the dead if not the beginning of a cult of the saints'. Although the plural of the noun **mneiâ** occurs nowhere else in the NT, 'sharing in the remembrance(s) of the saints' is grammatically possible and, although unique, may be the correct reading. See, for example, Heb. 13.7 and my notes on that verse in _Reading through Hebrews_.

'Cultivating', **diôkontes**, literally, 'pursuing'. As Chrysostom notes, 'he did not say "_doing_" it (**ergazomenoi**), but "pursuing" it, because he is teaching us not to wait for the needy to come to us but to run after them and track them down'. The hospitality of early Christians was famous. The pagan writer Lucian (_Peregrinus_ 13), indeed, mocked them for their gullibility, observing that any charlatan could impose on them and 'become very rich in a short time'.

14 Bless those who persecute you, bless and do not curse them. 15 Rejoice with those who rejoice, cry

with those who cry. 16 Have the same attitude towards one another, not thinking arrogant thoughts but associating with ordinary people. Do not be wise in your own estimation. 17 Repay no one with evil for evil, but take care [to do] what is good in the sight of everyone. 18 As far as you can, live in peace with all people. 19 Do not take revenge, beloved, but give place to the wrath [of God], for it is written, 'Vengeance is mine; I will repay,' says the Lord. 20 On the other hand, 'If your enemy is hungry, feed him; if he is thirsty, give him something to drink. For by doing this you will heap coals of fire on his head.' 21 Do not be overcome by evil, but overcome evil by good.

[14] This verse clearly comes from the Gospel tradition, since it recalls, as Barrett points out, the saying from the Sermon on the Mount expressed in Matt. 5.44 as 'Love your enemies, and pray for those who persecute you' and in Luke 6.27–28 as 'Love your enemies, do good to those who hate you, bless those who curse you, pray for those who insult you'. Paul incorporates elements from both versions. He often uses material which clearly comes from early accounts of the teaching of Jesus and which is found in the Gospels as we have them, as Sanday and Headlam demonstrate (381–2).

'Those who persecute', **tous diôkontas**, picks up **diôkontes** from the previous verse, but it obviously has a different sense.

[15] Chrysostom observes, with sharp insight into human psychology, that it is harder to rejoice with those who rejoice than to cry with those who cry; 'there is no one so hardhearted as not to weep over the one who is in trouble, but the other requires great nobility of soul, not only to keep from envying, but even to feel pleasure with the popular person. And that is why he has placed it first.'

[16] 'Have the same attitude', **to auto phronountes**, literally, 'thinking the same', is ambiguous. Does it mean 'have a common mind', i.e. 'think the same *as* everyone else', as Barrett takes it, or 'treat everyone the same way', i.e. 'think the same *of* everybody else'? Since Paul goes on to speak of mixing with all types of people, the latter is more likely: in other words, as the NEB (1961 edition) puts it, 'have equal regard for one another'. The second edition of the NEB altered this to 'Care as much about each other as about yourselves', which is quite a different thing, and not what Paul is talking about in this verse.

'Associating with ordinary people', **tois tapeinois synapagomenoi**, is another ambiguous expression. The Vulg. *humilibus consentientes* seems to take the participle **synapagomenoi** as meaning 'agreeing with'. It could also mean 'being carried away with', hence some commentators translate the phrase as 'giving yourselves over to humble tasks'. But this involves treating **tois tapeinois** as neuter, i.e. 'lowly *things*', although elsewhere in the NT it is masculine, i.e. 'lowly *people*', and the majority of scholars take this view. Incidentally, the NEB 'go about with *humble* folk' and Barrett 'keep company with the *humble*' perpetuate a traditional and archaic translation of **tapeinois**, which does not fit here. As Käsemann points out, the term refers to external need. The **tapeinoi** are those at the bottom of the pecking order in social terms, not those who behave in a 'humble' way, i.e. those who are are self-deprecating, and certainly not those resembling Uriah Heep. I translate **tois tapeinois** as 'ordinary people' with some misgiving, using a term which has become a common euphemism for 'the lower orders'. Chrysostom says of the phrase, 'bring yourself down to their lowly position, ride or walk with them; do not be humbled only mentally, but help them also and give them a hand'.

'Do not be wise in your own estimation' seems to be derived from Prov. 3.7.

[17] The thought expressed here seems to be another echo of some Gospel tradition. Compare Matt. 5.38–42 and Luke 6.29, 30.

'Take care [to do] what is good', **pronöoumenoi kala**, literally, 'providing good things'.

[18] 'As far as you can', literally, 'if possible on your part', in other words, 'as far as *you* can do anything about it'.

[19] 'Give place', **dote topon**, i.e. 'allow an opportunity', as in Eph. 4.27. Obviously Paul is not saying 'give in to your anger', so 'wrath', **orgêi**, here must be the judgment of God, and the meaning is 'leave it for God to deal with'. See note on 1.18.

'It is written', i.e. in Deut. 32.35. Note the redundant addition of 'says the Lord'. The same quotation occurs in Heb. 10.30 and, as I point out in my notes on that passage, does not come from our version of the Septuagint, which has 'on the day of vengeance' instead of 'vengeance is mine'.

[20] This is an accurate quotation from the Septuagint version of Prov. 25.21, 22.

'Coals of fire' are not the flames of hell but, according to such traditional commentators as Chrysostom, the pangs of conscience and shame which, hopefully, produce repentance and remorse in the wrongdoer. They cannot be the fiery punishment that God will inflict on him, since that would imply that we should take a malicious pleasure in seeing our enemy suffer, an idea which is totally at variance with the rest of this passage.

[21] This verse sums up the preceding section.

Chapter 13

1 Let every soul be subject to the superior authorities. For there is no authority which is not [appointed] by God, and those which exist have been appointed by God. 2 So anyone who sets himself up against the authority opposes God's ordinance, and those who oppose it shall bring down judgment against themselves. 3 For rulers are an object of fear to [those who do] evil deeds, not good ones. Do you want to avoid fear of the authority? Do good, and you will be praised by him. 4 For he is for you God's servant for a good purpose, but if you do wrong, beware, for he does not carry the sword for nothing. For he is God's servant when he inflicts punishment and retribution on the wrongdoer. 5 For this reason, one must be subject, not only because of retribution but for the sake of one's conscience. 6 Because of this also you should pay taxes, for they are God's ministers when they insist on this very thing. 7 Pay back to everybody what is due, to the one who [demands] tribute, tribute, to the one who [demands] tax, tax, to the one to whom fear [is due], fear, and to the one to whom respect [is due], respect.

This passage throws a great deal of light on the political and social background of the church at this period. One cannot assume, on the grounds that Paul is urging his audience to obey and respect the regime in power, that relations between the Roman authorities and the church were entirely harmonious at the time. The same exhortation to submit oneself to the ruling power was the theme of later Christians writing at a time when persecution had become the norm or had recently occurred, people such as Clement of Rome (I Clem. 60, 61), who still preached subordination to and co-operation with the authorities. Paul must have been particularly aware of the increasingly anti-authoritarian stance of his contemporaries in the Jewish communities, particularly in Judaea, which was soon to be engulfed by a disastrous and bloody war in 66. Paying tribute to the Roman authorities had presented the Jews for some years with a moral problem, as we know from many sources such as the Gospel accounts of the way in which this question was raised with Jesus (Matt. 22.17–22 and Luke 20.22–26). The Gentile Christians would probably have been surprised that the Jews had moral grounds for their reluctance to pay tax, but, like anyone else in the pagan community, would have come from a background where tax evasion was, if not normal, at least not an important moral issue. So, for both Jewish and Gentile Christians, Paul's exhortation was necessary.

[1] 'Authorities', **exousiais**, are clearly the political authorities. We can dismiss immediately the suggestion by a few commentators that it could refer to cosmic or supernatural powers. The fact that it does refer to such forces in Colossians and Ephesians is irrelevant here. The notion that all kings and rulers are appointed by God is common in Jewish literature and, as Sanday and Headlam point out, occurs in contexts where the writer is demonstrating that God is more powerful than any earthly ruler, and that rulers are responsible to God

for their actions. The idea that rulers are inviolable, beyond reproach, or even sacred because they are appointed by God is a much later distortion of Paul's message.

'Be subject', **hypotassesthô**, introduces a series of words which have the verb **tassô**, 'I order, appoint, ordain, assess (i.e. a tax)', as their root. The English translation, unfortunately, obscures the fact that this root occurs twice in this verse and twice in the next.

[2] 'Who sets himself up', **antitassomenos**, is the only instance of this verb being used by Paul.

'Judgment', **krima**, here is condemnation by a human court. It is not necessary to take it as referring to the final day of judgment.

[3] Due to the over-concise nature of the first sentence, early scribes have amended the text in various ways.

[4] 'For you', **soi**, is omitted in some manuscripts.

'When he inflicts punishment and retribution', **ekdikos eis orgên**, AV 'a revenger to execute wrath'.

[5] The appeal to conscience implies that the paying of taxes was already accepted as a moral imperative among the Christian community.

[6] 'Because of this also', i.e. for the sake of one's conscience.

'Ministers', **leitourgoi**, is a common term for any public servant or administrator.

'When they insist on', **proskarterountes**, literally, 'persevering' or 'taking pains over'.

[7] 'Tribute', **phoron**, and 'tax', **telos**, are not easy to distinguish. Commentators have generally explained the former as the tribute paid by a subject nation, but, to be more

accurate, it is the poll tax levied on individuals in that state. It is significant that in the passages referred to above Matthew has **kênson** where Luke has **phoron**. The **kênsos** was assessed on the basis of information supplied by the census-returns in the provinces, as its name indicates, and, when collected, after the appropriate deductions had disappeared into the pockets of the tax collectors, made up the *tributum*, i.e. **phoros**. **Telos** probably refers to customs duties or sale taxes, in other words, indirect taxes.

8 Owe no one anything except the love [which you owe] one another; for he who loves his neighbour has fulfilled the Law. 9 For the [commandments] 'You shall not commit adultery, you shall not murder, you shall not steal, you shall not covet', and any other commandment are summed up in this [one] sentence, 'You shall love your neighbour as yourself.' 10 Love does nothing evil to one's neighbour, so love is the fulfilment of the Law. 11 This especially, because you know the time, that it is the hour already for you to awake from sleep, for our salvation is now nearer than [it was] when we [first] believed. 12 The night is far spent, the day is at hand. So let us put off the works of darkness and put on the armour of light. 13 Let us live decent lives, as in the daytime, not in revelry and drinking, not in sexual activities and outrageous behaviour, not in strife and rivalry, 14 but put on the Lord Jesus Christ and have no concern for the flesh and its desires.

[8] The thought behind this concise verse is not immediately obvious. The first part is clear, because it sums up the theme of the previous verse, i.e. 'pay everybody what is due to them',

and then, almost as an afterthought, Paul says, 'But there is one thing you *do* owe everybody, and that is love, and among Christians that means love for one another', or as Barrett puts it, 'the only debt Christians ought to incur is that which they are bound to incur and can never completely discharge – the debt of mutual love.'

'Owe', **opheilete**, can in grammar be either a statement or an imperative, i.e. it can be translated as 'owe' or 'you do owe', and also the verb can mean 'ought' as well as 'owe'. I have restored the suppressed second **opheilete**, '[which *you owe*]', as a statement. Alternatively, it has been suggested that 'except', **ei mê**, literally, 'if not', can be translated as 'but', and then the passage would mean, 'owe no one anything – but *you ought* to love one another'.

'Has fulfilled the Law', **nomon peplêrôken**, uses the perfect tense, as does the parallel passage in Gal. 5.14, 'For the fulfilment of the whole Law is expressed in one statement – "you shall love your neighbour as yourself".' As in Galatians, Paul clearly has in his mind the Gospel accounts of Jesus' reply to the lawyer (Matt. 22.34–40; Mark 12.28–34 and Luke 10.25–28). The reference to 'the Law' brings us back to Paul's earlier theme of the relevance of the *Torah*.

The references to the Mosaic commandments in the next verse, as Käsemann and others point out, make it impossible to take **nomon** here in the sense of 'the general moral law'. Incidentally, because the phrase **ton heteron**, literally, 'the other', translated here as 'neighbour', comes immediately before **nomon**, there have been attempts to attach it to the noun and produce the translation 'the other (or 'the rest of') law', but this suggestion must be rejected. The Vulg. *qui enim diligit proximum, legem implevit* makes the meaning clear.

[9] 'Are summed up', **anakephalaioutai**, a verb which has as its core the noun **kephalê**, 'head', is found in only one other place in the NT, Eph. 1.10, 'so that he might sum up in Christ

everything in heaven and earth', where it means both that everything is summed up under one heading, and also that it is placed under one Head. Here Paul is saying that the individual commandments can be put under one heading, 'you shall love your neighbour as yourself'. The Law, in fact, *can* be fulfilled, but only by the exercise of love.

The order of the commandments differs from Ex. 20.13–17 and Deut. 5.17–21 (Sept.), but as the Exodus and Deuteronomy passages also differ from each other, this is hardly surprising. Some manuscripts include 'bearing false witness', which is in the Exodus and Deuteronomy list, but the best ones do not have it. The order given here, leaving aside the omission of 'bearing false witness', is that which we find also in Luke 18.20, except that Luke refers to honouring one's parents rather than covetousness, and in Philo (*On the Ten Commandments*, 51). The final quotation in this verse is from Lev. 19.18, and, as we have seen, occurs also in the Galatians passage quoted above and elswhere in the NT.

[10] 'Love is the fulfilment of the Law' repeats and sums up the statement in v. 8.

[11] 'This especially', **kai touto**, literally, 'and this', is not the object of **eidotes**, 'knowing', but refers back to the exhortation to love one's neighbour.

'Time', **kairon**, is a difficult word to pin down. In Gal. 6.9 it means something like 'season', and in Gal. 6.10, 'chance' or 'opportunity'. There is frequently a notion in this word of 'the right time', hence the NEB translates 'because you know the time', **eidotes ton kairon**, literally, 'knowing the time', as 'remember how critical the moment is'.

'You', **hûmâs**, is better than 'us', **hêmâs**, which, probably because 'our' occurs later in this verse, is found in many manuscripts. These two pronouns are also frequently confused because their pronunciation was identical in later Greek.

'Salvation' is our final redemption, which is obviously nearer now than it was at the time when we first believed in the gospel of Christ.

[12] 'Is far spent', **proëkopsen**, the familiar AV translation which is difficult to improve on. **Prokoptô**, a verb which comes from a military background, means literally, 'to cut one's way forward'. In Gal. 1.14 it is used by Paul to describe his enthusiasm as a Pharisee, 'I *outstripped* in my orthodoxy many contemporaries'.

'The works of darkness', which are clearly the same as 'the works of the flesh' referred to in Gal. 5.19, are the activities characteristic of a life lived 'according to the flesh', as distinct from the 'armour of light', the new life which is 'according to the Spirit', and which Paul refers to in Gal. 5.22 as 'the fruits of the Spirit'. 'Armour' is used here to make the point that the Christian life is a life of conflict and struggle against evil forces.

Some commentators, who pursue the metaphor of clothing further than Paul ever intended, see 'the works of darkness' as some sort of night attire. Sanday and Headlam, for instance, refer coyly to 'uncomely garments of the night'. Threadbare pyjamas, I presume?

[13] Compare this verse with Gal. 5.19–21. My notes in *Reading through Galatians* refer to several of the words which Paul uses here. Incidentally, as many commentators note, this and the next verse are the famous texts which marked the conversion of Augustine (*Confessions*, 8.12).

'Let us live decent lives', **euschêmonôs peripatêsômen**, literally. 'let us walk decorously'.

'As in the daytime', in other words, 'since you are children of light not of darkness'.

'Revelry', **kômois**, and 'drinking', **methais**, are also associated in Gal. 5.21. Paul is not referring merely to parties, but to the festivities connected with pagan festivals.

'Sexual activities', **koitais**, literally, 'beds'.

'Outrageous behavour', **aselgeiais**, could refer to hooliganism or acts of wanton violence, not necessarily those involving sex.

'Strife', **eridi**, and 'rivalry', **zêlôi**, are another pair of vices found in association in the Galatians passage, and also in II Cor. 12.20.

[14] 'Put on the Lord Jesus Christ' is a striking metaphor which goes beyond the simple idea of putting on clothes. Gal. 3.27. 'For all of you who have been baptized into Christ have put on Christ', would indicate a connection here with baptism, but the metaphor 'put on' is common in other contexts, as I point out in my notes on that verse. 'Put on' here is almost the same as 'become like' or even 'turn into'.

'Concern', **pronoian**, literally, 'forethought'.

Chapter 14

1 Accept anyone who is weak in faith, [and] do not [get involved] in the settling of arguments. 2 One person believes he can eat everything, while another, being weak, eats vegetables. 3 The one who eats [everything] should not look down on the one who does not, and the one who does not eat [everything] should not judge the one who does, for God has accepted him. 4 Who are you to judge another man's servant? It is his own Master's concern whether he stands or falls; and he will stand, for his Master can make him stand.

[1] The person who is 'weak in faith' is the Christian who has scruples about practices which the 'strong', i.e. the one who does not share these scruples, accepts as normal.

There has been a great deal of discussion among commentators whether Paul is thinking particularly of Jewish Christians or of some other group who abstained from certain foods. Jerome states that the 'weak' are those who avoided the meat sold in the markets 'at that time', because they believed that it would cause pollution due to its connection with idolatry. He also puts forward the strange view that the 'strong' are those who eat meat 'without moderation', *immoderate*, i.e. too much meat or perhaps too much of the

wrong kind of meat. This seems to go with another suggestion
in his commentary that the 'weak' is to be defined as *infirmus
aut aetate aut corporis calore*, 'weak either because of age or
the heat of his body', in other words one who is medically
infirm. Jerome recognizes that other commentators (*ut qui-
dam putant*, 'as some think') interpret the passage as referring
to Jews, but rejects any connection with the Mosaic Law. This
is inconsisent with his remark in *Against Jovinianus*, II, 16,
that Paul 'is speaking against those who, while believing in
Christ, were still practising Judaism', *contra eos loquitur, qui
in Christum credentes, adhuc iudaizabant.*

The fact that abstention from wine is mentioned in v. 21 has
led some commentators to assume that the abstainers cannot
be orthodox Jews, since such a practice is not one normally
found among them. Paul seems to be referring to it, almost in
passing, as an example of the sort of thing that can cause
problems. I would, however, suggest that abstention from
wine may have been the practice of orthodox Jews living at
that time in a Gentile society, where they regarded the wine as
ritually impure for some reason which we do not know,
possibly because the various stages in its production were
celebrated by pagan rites.

It has also been claimed that the reference to vegetarianism
proves that they are not Jews. Again the argument is dubious:
eating vegetables could be a way of avoiding problems when
eating with Gentile Christians. They may even have avoided
meat all the time because they lived amongst people whose
treatment of meat was not according to Jewish practice.
Where most meat on sale in the market has been connected
with pagan sacrifice or has not been correctly slaughtered, the
safest thing to do would be to abstain from it all together. It
may be that we are dealing with some Essene sect of Judaism,
but there is no need to reject the obvious conclusion that the
'weak' here are those Jewish or Judaizing Christians who have
retained certain scruples appropriate to their former religion.

There is certainly no evidence for the popular notion that Paul is referring here to the practices of some Gnostic or semi-pagan sect. His tone is too moderate and sympathetic for that.

'Accept', **proslambanesthe**, literally, 'take in', 'receive besides'. This verb occurs again in v. 3.

'Do not [get involved] in the settling of arguments', **mê eis diakriseis dialogismôn**, literally, 'not to judgments between debates'. The NEB has 'without attempting to settle doubtful points'.

[2] 'Believes', **pisteuei**, is, of course, cognate with 'faith', **pistis**, and probably means something like 'has enough faith that'. Barrett translates the first part of this verse as, 'one man has faith so strong that he can and does eat all things'.

[3] 'Should not look down on', **mê exoutheneitô**, literally, 'let him not treat as nothing'. This verb is repeated in v. 10.

[4] 'Master' in this verse, of course, is the same word as the one we normally translate as 'Lord', i.e. **kûrios**.

'Stands' can be taken in two ways, remaining upright throughout the troubles and trials of this life, and also standing uncondemned before the judgment seat of God.

5 For one man distinguishes between one day and another, another man judges every day [the same]; let each one be fully assured in his own mind. 6 The one who is concerned about the day, is concerned for the Lord; the one who eats, eats for the Lord, for he gives thanks to God; and the one who does not eat, does not eat for the Lord and gives thanks to God. 7 For none of us lives for himself or dies for himself. 8 For if we live, we live for the Lord, and if we die, we die for the

Lord. So whether we live or whether we die, we are the Lord's. 9 For this was the purpose for which Christ died and lived, [namely,] that he should be Master of both the dead and the living. 10 Why do you judge your brother, and why do you look down on him, since we shall all stand before the judgment seat of God? 11 For it is written, '[As] I live (says the Lord), it is to me that every knee shall bow and every tongue give praise to God.' 12 So then, each one of us shall give an account of himself to God.

[5] Paul is clearly speaking about the observance of a ritual calendar. It could refer simply to keeping the sabbath, but it probably includes the observance of new moons and the Jewish festivals, as in Gal. 4.10, 'you observe days, months, seasons and years', and in Col. 2.16, 'so let no one judge you in the matter of food and drink, or in respect of a feast, a new moon or sabbaths'. In all these cases we are dealing with some form of Judaism.

'Distinguishes' and 'judges' in this verse are the same verb, **krînei**, which in the latter instance carries the meaning 'judge in favour of'.

'Be fully assured', **plêrophoreisthô**; see note on 4.21.

[6] Paul is saying here that both the person who has scruples and the one who does not, do what they do as their service to God. The one who eats something which the other will not eat thanks God for his food, while the one who does not eat still gives thanks to God. Barrett translates the last part as, 'he who abstains, abstains to the Lord, and over his meal (of vegetables) he gives thanks to God', but it is unnecessary to assume that the abstainer has to eat something in order to thank God, and it is not what Paul actually says.

[7, 8] The point being made here is that we are not isolated or self-contained entities existing in our own right; our lives and our deaths are in the hands of God – they are not under our control.

[9] There are great subtleties in this verse, which at first sight seems to be saying simply that Christ tasted death in order to become the Lord of the dead, and that he 'lived', i.e. was incarnated as a human being in order to become Lord of the living. 'Lived', however, refers to his resurrection, when he became alive again after death, since the normal order – lived, died, and living, dead – has been inverted. Compare Rev. 1.18, 'I was dead and, look, I am alive for ever and ever, and I hold the keys of death and Hades', and Rev. 2.8, 'Thus speaks the first and the last, who was dead and lived'. 'Lived', **ezêsen**, means, in effect, 'became alive', which it also means in Rev. 2.8.

[10] 'Judgment seat', **bêmati**, is frequently found in Acts as the term for the raised place from which a king or magistrate presided over a court. Note that in II Cor. 5.10 Paul refers to the judgment seat of Christ, and some manuscripts, followed by the AV, have 'of Christ' here instead of 'of God', but there is no need to alter the text; God, as Sanday and Headlam point out, judges the world through Christ.

[11] The quotation is from Isa. 45.23 (Sept.), and Paul has substituted 'I live', **zô egô**, for 'I swear by myself', omitted 'surely righteousness shall come forth from my mouth, my words shall not be turned away', and then continued with the rest of the verse. Hence we have to add 'as' in order to make the opening verb into an oath-like affirmation. Note that in Phil. 2.10 it is 'at the name of Jesus' that 'every knee shall bow'.

'[Shall] give praise', **exomologêsetai**, literally, 'will confess, acknowledge'. In the Septuagint, however, this verb is often used in the sense of 'to make grateful acknowledgment', hence 'to give thanks and praise'.

[12] 'Shall give an account', **logon dôsei**, is a legal term.

13 Let us, therefore, not judge one another, but rather come to the decision that we do not put an obstacle or stumbling block in our brother's way. 14 I know and am persuaded by the Lord Jesus that there is nothing unclean of itself, except when someone reckons that it is unclean, and then it is unclean to him. 15 For if your brother is upset by your food, you are no longer acting with love. Do not destroy by your food the one for whom Christ died. 16 Do not, therefore, let what is good for you be something to be spoken badly of. 17 For the kingdom of God is not food or drink, but righteousness, peace and joy in the Holy Spirit.

[13] 'Judge' and 'come to a decision' are both from the same verb, **krînô**, which, as in v. 5, carries different meanings.

　　'Obstacle', **proskomma**, and 'stumbling block', **skandalon**, as in 9.33, are virtually synonyms; they are the things which impede the progress of our Christian brothers and sisters.

[14] 'Unclean', **koinon**, literally, 'common', hence 'profane'. In the NT this adjective is used frequently to denote objects which are ritually impure, most famously in the story of Peter's vision in Acts 10, when he is urged to eat all kinds of forbidden animals, but replies, 'Certainly not, Lord, because I have never eaten anything *unclean* (**koinon**) or *impure* (**akatharton**).'

[15] 'You are no longer acting with love', literally, 'you are no longer walking according to love'. This assumes, of course, that you know what effect your eating of forbidden food has on your brother, yet you persist in eating it. Obviously your brother is irritated by your breaking of conventions, but if you encourage him against his better judgment to follow your example, and as a result cause him to have a bad conscience, it is far worse.

[16] 'What is good for you', literally, 'your good', which most probably is your freedom in Christ to eat anything, or possibly the good food you have been allowed to eat. Käsemann suggests that it is 'the state of salvation'.

[17] 'Kingdom of God' here seems to refer to the present state of the Christian and, as Col. 1.13 and Eph. 1.3 and 2.6 imply, it is a kingdom which already exists. Elsewhere Paul uses the term as though it were something which has still to come about, or, as he often says (e.g. Gal. 5.21, Eph. 5.5 and I Cor. 6.9), something to be inherited. This ambivalence reflects the use of the term by Jesus himself.

'Peace' and 'joy' are described in Gal. 5.22 as the 'fruit of the Spirit'.

18 For he who serves Christ in this way is well-pleasing to God and esteemed by mankind. 19 So let us then pursue the things that make for peace and for the building up of one another. 20 Do not destroy the work of God for the sake of food. Everything is pure, but it is wrong when the one who eats causes someone to stumble. 21 It is good neither to eat meat nor to drink wine, nor [to do anything] which causes your brother to stumble. 22 Keep before God the faith which you keep in yourself. Blessed is the one who

finds nothing to criticize himself for in the matter which is under scrutiny. 23 If the one who has doubts eats, he has incurred judgment, because [he is doing it] not from faith, and everything which is not from faith is sin.

[18] 'Esteemed', **dokimos**, i.e. 'tried and approved'.

[19] 'The things that make for peace', **ta tês eirênês**, literally, 'the things of peace'.

'Building up' is a complex metaphor which reflects Paul's concept of the church as the body of Christ and at the same time as a holy temple. The emphasis is on the corporate building, not on individual edification.

[20] 'The work of God', to continue with the corporate image, is more likely to be the church or the Christian community, rather than an individual Christian.

The second part of this verse is not easy to follow. Literally, it means 'all things are pure, but [it is] evil to the man who eats through an obstacle/stumbling block'. We can be sure that the singular word 'evil', **kakon**, refers to the act of eating, not to the food itself, i.e. 'everything', because the Greek word for 'everything' is plural, i.e. 'all things', **panta**. But who is in the wrong? Is it the one who sets the example of eating forbidden food, or the one who follows his example? The former is supported by the NEB version, 'Everything is pure in itself, but anything is bad for the man who *by his eating causes another to fall*', and Barrett, 'All things are clean; but they work harm to the man *who eats them so as to cause offence*'. The Rheims version translates the phrase 'through an obstacle', **dia proskommatos**, Vulg. *per offendiculum*, as 'by giving offence', which agrees with the NEB and Barrett. On the other hand, Tyndale has 'with hurt of his conscience', which was followed by Cranmer, and clearly sees the harm as coming to the one who follows the example. The Geneva and AV have 'with offence', which is ambivalent. It is clear that both the one who sets the example and the one whose conscience is made to feel guilty when he follows the example are harmed. As Barrett suggests, the obscurity of this sentence is perhaps due to the fact that Paul was thinking of the harm caused to both parties.

[21] Paul is suggesting not that everyone has to be an abstainer and a vegetarian all the time, but only on occasion. The infinitives 'to eat' and 'to drink', as Barrett points out, are aorists and refer to specific actions, not repeated ones.

[22] The first part of this verse is another ambiguous sentence. The AV 'Hast thou faith? have it to thyself before God' is based on a poor text which did not have the relative pronoun 'which'. The text which I have used could also be translated, 'Keep to yourself before God the faith which you have'. The general message seems to be, 'You may feel that it is perfectly all right for you to eat the food which causes the problem, but to avoid harming your brother's conscience, refrain from it. Do not, for the sake of maintaining a principle, continue to eat it. God knows your beliefs about this issue – you do not need to make a public display of them.'

'The one who finds nothing to criticize himself for', **ho mê krînôn heauton**, literally, 'the one not judging himself'. Note again that this verb can mean more than simply 'judge'. Barrett takes this phrase as meaning 'he who does not waver', on the grounds that it corresponds to **ho diakrînomenos**, 'the one who has doubts', i.e. 'the one who wavers', in the next verse, but this is straying too far away from the meaning.

'In the matter which is under scrutiny', **en hôi dokimazei**, literally, 'in [a matter] which he scrutinizes'. The problem here is the ambiguity of the verb **dokimazei**, which has the basic meaning 'to test', 'to make trial of' or 'to examine', but sometimes means 'to approve after testing'. So here the phrase could mean something like 'in a issue where your conscience approves of what you are doing'. The basic message, however, is clear, whichever meaning of the verb we accept: 'you are fortunate if you have a clear conscience in such matters'.

[23] 'He has incurred judgment', **katakekritai**, literally, 'he has been judged' or 'he has been condemned'.

'Everything which is not from faith is sin', i.e. 'any act which violates one's beliefs is sinful'. In other words, if one does something while believing it to be wrong it is a sin. As Chrysostom says, 'When a person neither feels sure nor believes that a thing is clean, how has he not sinned?' Augustine (*Against Julian*, IV, 32) uses this text to argue that even the good deeds of non-believers are automatically sinful, because they have an unbelieving will, and concludes, 'For everything which is not from faith, whether you will or not, is sin', *omne enim, velis nolis, quod non est ex fide, peccatum est*. Needless to say, this is not what Paul is saying, as Chrysostom quietly reminds us, 'Now all which Paul has said refers to this subject, not to everything.'

Chapter 15

1 We who are strong ought to bear the weaknesses of those who are not strong, and not please ourselves. 2 Let each one of us please his neighbour for his good and for the building up [of one another]. 3 For Christ did not please himself, but, as it is written, 'the reproaches of those reproaching you fell upon me'. 4 For all which was written beforehand, was written for our instruction, so that we might have hope through our patience and through the encouragement of the scriptures. 5 May the God of patience and encouragement grant that you share the same mind in [your dealings with] one another in accordance with Christ Jesus, 6 so that with one heart and with one mouth you may glorify the God and Father of our Lord Jesus Christ.

[1] Paul sums up his previous argument and concludes that we should put the needs of others first.

'Bear the weaknesses', **ta asthenêmata bastazein**, is an ambiguous phrase: firstly, it obviously refers to the previous chapter's subject, i.e. the acceptance of the scruples of the 'weak'; and secondly, it introduces a different theme, the carrying of the burdens of those who need your help. Compare Gal. 6.2, 'Bear one another's burdens', **allêlôn ta**

barê bastazete. Paul is making a connection between accommodating the scruples of those whose consciences are weak and the general principle that we should carry one another's burdens. **Asthenêmata**, 'weaknesses', can also be physical ailments or illnesses.

[2] 'For his good' is added to modify the notion that 'pleasing' one's neighbour is sufficient in itself. As the use of the term **anthrôpareskoi**, 'man-pleasers', in Col. 3.22 and Eph. 6.6 makes clear, 'pleasing' people is not necessarily a good thing.

'Building up'; see note on 14.19.

[3] The quotation is from Ps. 69.9 (Sept. 68.10), a Psalm famous for its prophecies of the sufferings of Christ, for example, 'for my thirst they gave me vinegar to drink'. It is particularly appropriate that this quotation is preceded in the original by the words, 'since the zeal of your house has devoured me'.

[4] The quotation in the previous verse leads Paul to insert a reminder of the importance of the OT scriptures in pointing to the redemption of the world by Jesus Christ. 'Hope', as I argue in my notes on 8.24, is almost a synonym for 'faith'.

'Through our patience', literally, 'through *the* patience', seems awkwardly joined with 'through the encouragement of the scriptures'. The statement, as often happens, has been abbreviated. Paul seems to be saying that, firstly, we should wait patiently for the fulfilment of our hopes, and secondly, we should be encouraged in those hopes by what the scriptures have prophesied about Christ. The association of 'hope' and 'patience' recalls 8.25, 'If we hope for something we cannot see, we wait for it with patience.'

'Encouragement', **paraklêseôs**, AV 'comfort', is more than the emotional boost gained from reading uplifting thoughts; it is the knowledge and realization that God's plan to redeem the world through the incarnation, death and resurrection of his son is revealed in the scriptures. Barrett believes that the scriptures refer to the lot of the Christian, 'because Scripture, *by foretelling our situation*, encourages us to pass through it in hope', but this is unlikely here in view of the Messianic context of the previous verse. **Paraklêsis** is related to the verb **parakaleô** and to the epithet of the Holy Spirit, **paraklêtos**, for which see my notes on 12.8. The AV 'comfort' nowadays carries a much weaker sense than it did in the seventeenth century. 'Encouragement' as a translation is only slightly better; we have no word which conveys the full sense of **paraklêsis** as an activity which affects the intellect as well as the emotions.

[5] Paul interjects a prayer incorporating the previous verse's reference to 'patience' and 'encouragement'. It seems to be a spontaneous blessing emerging from the context, rather as the prayer in v. 13, 'May the God of hope . . .,' picks up the reference to hope in v. 12.

'In [your dealings with] one another', **en allêlois**, rather than 'with one another' (NEB). Compare 12.16, 'have the same attitude *towards one another* (**eis allêlous**)', and see my notes on that verse. Paul is making the point here and in the following verses that in the Christian community Jews and Christians, or the 'weak' and the 'strong', should be united in following the example of Jesus and in our worship of God; he is not saying that we should think the same thoughts as everybody else.

[6] 'With one heart', **homothûmadon**, i.e. 'with the same soul'.

'The God and Father of our Lord Jesus Christ' is the obvious translation of this phrase. It is a distortion of the Greek to translate it as 'God, the Father of our Lord Jesus

Christ' in order to avoid saying that God is the God of Jesus Christ. In John 20.17 the risen Christ says, 'I am ascending to my Father and your Father, to my God and your God.' See my notes on the same phrase in Eph. 1.3 in *Reading through Colossians and Ephesians*.

7 So accept one another, as Christ accepted you to God's glory. 8 For I say that Christ has been made a minister of the circumcision for God's truth, in order to confirm the promises of [our] fathers, 9 and so that the Gentiles may glorify God for his mercy, as it is written, 'Therefore I shall confess you among the nations and sing praises to your name.' 10 And again he says, 'Rejoice, nations, with his people,' 11 and again, 'Praise the Lord, all you nations, and let all the peoples praise him.' 12 And again Isaiah says, 'There shall be the root of Jesse, and the one who rises up to rule the nations; in him shall the nations hope.'

[7] 'Accept', **proslambanesthe**, was used to introduce the theme of the previous chapter and is clearly intended to reinforce the message of that chapter.

Does 'to God's glory' go with 'so accept one another', or with 'as Christ accepted you'? It could be both, since we glorify God when we accept one another, just as it was 'to God's glory' that Christ has welcomed everyone, Jew and Gentile alike, into the kingdom of heaven. It is also possible that 'to God's glory', **eis doxan tou Theou**, means '*into* God's glory', i.e. 'into his glorious kingdom' or 'to share in his glory'.

[8] 'Minister of the circumcision', i.e. a servant of the circumcised Jews. Christ, as Gal. 4.4, 5 says, was 'born of a

woman, born under the Law, in order to redeem those under the Law, so that we might take up our adoption'. The process of redemption had to start with the 'circumcision', i.e. those under the Law, as the scriptures had prophesied. Chrysostom explains the phrase as follows: 'By having come and fulfilled the Law, and been circumcised, having been born of the seed of Abraham, he undid the curse, stayed the anger of God, and made those who were to receive the promises fit for them.' Christ submitted to the Law by becoming a Jew. Barrett not only misses the point of this verse but also makes the inappropriate observation that Christ became a servant of the Jews, 'who, especially when described as the "circumcision", may be regarded as the most awkward and irritating of scrupulous persons. He thus provides an example for all strong Christians.'

'For God's truth', i.e. to demonstrate the truth of God's promises and his word as revealed in scripture. 'Truth' also carries the sense of 'righteousness' or 'righteous judgment'. See my notes on 2.8.

'Confirm', **bebaiôsai**, literally, 'make firm', that is, 'establish', 'guarantee', and hence, 'fufil'.

'The promises of [our] fathers' are principally the promises God made to Abraham, but they include all those statements in the OT which refer to God's promises to his people.

[9] The grammatical structure of this sentence is a little shaky, but the meaning is clear. The prophecies of scripture apply to Gentiles as well as Jews, as Paul demonstrates with a series of quotations from the Septuagint which have obviously been selected to act as proof texts. The scriptural references in this and the next three verses to Gentiles and Jews being united in their worship of God recall an earlier theme, particularly that covered in chapters 9–11. Note, of course, that 'Gentiles' and 'nations' are the same word in Greek, i.e. **ethnê**.

'I shall confess', **exomologêsomai**, or 'I shall praise'; see the note on 14.11. This quotation is from Ps. 18.49 (Sept. 17.50).

'Sing praises', **psalô**, literally, 'pluck', i.e. play on a stringed instrument. This is, of course, the derivation of the word 'psalm'.

[10] This is from Deut. 32.43.

[11] This is from Ps. 117.1 (Sept. 116.1), with minor variations in word order and vocabulary.

[12] This quotation is taken from Isa. 11.10. Jesse, of course, is the father of David from whom Jesus is descended. See the note on 1.2, 3.

'The one who rises up', **ho anistamenos**, is not just 'the one who appears' or 'the one who springs from that ancestor'; for Christians he is also 'the one who is resurrected'.

13 May the God of hope fill you with all joy and peace in your faith, so that you overflow with hope by the power of the Holy Spirit. 14 I am convinced, my brothers and sisters, yes, I, too, [am convinced when I think] of you, that you also are full of goodness, filled with all knowledge and also able to teach one another. 15 But, on some of the subjects where I have been refreshing your memory, I have written to you in rather bold terms because of the grace which has been given to me by God 16 to be a minister of Christ Jesus among the Gentiles, acting like a priest in regard to the gospel of God, so that the offering of the Gentiles should be well received, sanctified by the Holy Spirit.

[13] This prayer marks the transition from the main body of the letter to the final section.

'In your faith', literally, 'in believing', **en tôi pisteuein**.

'Overflow', one of Paul's favourite words, **perisseuein**, which he has used in 3.7 and 5.15. This abundance is the manifestation of God's lavish grace, as in Eph. 1.7, 8, 'according to the wealth of his grace, which he *poured out abundantly* (**eperisseusen**) on us with all wisdom and judgment'.

[14] 'Yes, I, too', **kai autos egô**, is added to assure his audience that he supports them and that they should not be offended by anything he has said. It is similar to the beginning of chapter 10 of II Corinthians, 'I myself, I, Paul, beseech you'. A more abrasive type of personal reference can be seen in Gal. 5.2, 'Look, I, Paul, am telling you'.

'[When I think] of you', literally, 'concerning you'.

'Full', **mestoi**, and 'filled', **peplêrômenoi**, continue the image of 'overflow' in the previous verse.

'Goodness', **agathôsynês**, only occurs four times in the NT. In Gal. 5.22 it is described as a 'fruit of the Spirit' and in Eph. 5.9 as a 'fruit of light'. **Agathôsynê** is sheer goodness, a state which can only be given by God and which is manifested by those whose actions are entirely motivated by love. It is significant that some manuscripts substitute 'love', **agapês**, for this word.

'Teach', **nouthetein**, literally, 'put in mind'. It tends to mean 'chastise' or 'rebuke', hence the AV 'admonish'. The NEB 'give advice' is better, but the reference to 'all knowledge' would indicate that Paul is thinking of a wider range of communication.

[15] 'On some of the subjects', **apo merous**, literally, 'in part', i.e. 'not throughout my letter but only in some places'.

'Where I have been refreshing your memory', **hôs epana-**

mimnêiskôn hûmâs, literally, 'as reminding you again'. Paul diplomatically implies that his audience already knew the points he has made in his letter, but it is clear from this remark that he was concerned that they did not fully appreciate the importance of some issues.

[16] Reading between the lines, it is clear from the carefully structured statements in this and the previous verse that Paul was particularly anxious to establish with his Roman audience the need to accept the Gentile Christians as full members of the church and to abandon any attempt to make them conform to a Judaizing form of Christianity. Paul excuses himself for the boldness of some of his remarks on the grounds that he was appointed by God as the apostle to the Gentiles because God wanted the Gentiles to be included in the new covenant. There is a scarcely veiled hint that his authority comes from God and that those who do not accept what he says are resisting God's will. Is Paul addressing the Jewish or the Gentile members of his audience? Both, since he is warning some and assuring others at the same time.

'Acting like a priest', **hierourgounta**, a word found nowhere else in the NT, has been deliberately chosen to link the new covenant to the old dispensation of the Law where the priests mediated between God and Israel. Paul's ministry as the apostle of the gospel to the Gentiles has taken the place of any previous priestly ministry. He is, in effect, claiming to be the priest of God in preaching the gospel to the Gentiles.

'Offering', **prosphorâ**, continues the image of the priest making an offering in the Temple. The image of the Christian believer as a sacrifice offered to God was found in 12.1, 'present your bodies as a living, holy sacrifice, well-pleasing to God'. See the notes on that verse.

'Sanctified', **hêgiasmenê**, because only a 'holy' and 'blameless' sacrifice could be offered to God according to the Law.

Note, incidentally, the reference to all the persons of the Holy Trinity in this verse.

17 So in matters relating to God I can boast of Christ Jesus. 18 For I will not be so bold as to mention any of those things which Christ did not achieve through me in word and in deed in regard to the response of the Gentiles, 19 in the power of signs and wonders, in the power of the Spirit, with the result that I have completed [the preaching of] the gospel of Christ in a circle from Jerusalem as far round as Illyricum, 20 but I have made it my aim to preach the gospel only where Christ's name has not been heard, in such a way as not to build on another's foundations, 21 but as it is written, 'Those to whom no report of him was given, shall see, and those who have not heard, shall understand.'

[17] 'In matters relating to God', **ta pros ton Theon**, as we can see from the use of the phrase in Heb. 2.17 and Heb. 5.1, refers to the functions of the priest in the Temple, the matters which he has to deal with in carrying out his duties. In Paul's case it is a metaphor for the work as an apostle for which he has been ordained by God, 'acting like a priest in regard to the gospel'. It is not to be translated merely as 'in my relationship with God' or 'as far as God is concerned'.

'I can boast of Christ Jesus', literally, 'I have boasting in Christ Jesus', **echô kauchêsin en Christôi Iêsou**. Compare Gal. 6.14, 'Far be it from me to boast except of the cross of our Lord Jesus Christ.' The expression **kauchêsin echô** has the same meaning as **kauchêma echô**, which occurs in 4.2, where I translate **echei kauchêma** as 'he has something to boast about'. 'Boasting' does not always carry a negative sense, as we have seen in 2.17 and elsewhere; in fact, in Paul it more frequently has a good sense, i.e. being proud of something one should take pride in. See my notes on Gal. 6.4 and 6.14 in *Reading through Galatians*. Paul is saying here that Christ is all-sufficient and that he is proud to put his trust in him and not in the rituals laid down by the Mosaic Law.

[18] The double negatives obscure the meaning. We could translate the first part of this verse as, 'For I will dare to speak *only* of those things which Christ *did* achieve through me.' The sentence is also too concise; Paul seems to be saying two things: firstly, 'I cannot claim the credit for anything I did, because it was Christ who acted through me'; and secondly, 'I would not presume to speak of the achievements of other evangelists.'

'In word and in deed', i.e. both in preaching and in such acts as the blinding of Elymas the sorcerer (Acts 13.11), the healing of the cripple at Lystra (Acts 14.8–11) and the miracles in Ephesus (Acts 19.12).

'The response', **hypakoên**, i.e. 'hearing, believing and obeying'. See the notes on 1.5 and 6.16.

[19] 'Power' is repeated because the 'signs and wonders' are a manifestation of the power of the Spirit. The AV 'of the Spirit of God' is due to a variant reading in some manuscripts. Other manuscripts read 'of the Holy Spirit', followed by the NEB.

'Circle' is not quite accurate; it is more of an arc. Paul is not recorded as active in Egypt or Cyrene. Jerusalem roughly represents one end of the arc, and Illyricum (the Balkans) the other. Some commentators are concerned about the precision of Paul's statement, but Paul is not giving a detailed account.

[20] 'I have made it my aim', literally, 'making it a point of honour', **philotîmoumenon**, hence 'striving eagerly', 'aspiring'.

'Only where Christ's name has not been heard', literally, 'not where Christ has been named'.

[21] This is an accurate quotation from the Septuagint version of Isa. 52.15, a verse which introduces the well-known song of the Suffering Servant in chapter 53.

22 Because of this I have been prevented from visiting you many times. 23 But now, since there is no more scope for me in this area, and I have had for many years a longing to visit you, 24 [I shall do so] whenever I travel to Spain. For I hope on my way through to see you and to be helped by you on my way there, if I can first to some extent have my fill of your company. 25 I am now travelling to Jerusalem in the service of the saints. 26 For Macedonia and Achaea have decided to make a contribution to the poor among the saints in Jerusalem. 27 Yes, they have decided, and they do owe them something, for if the Gentiles have shared in their spiritual blessings they ought also to minister to their physical needs. 28 So when I have finished this [task] and completed the delivery of these proceeds to them, I shall come by you on my way to Spain. 29 I know that when I visit you I shall come with the full blessing of Christ.

[22] 'I have been prevented', **enekoptomên**, from **engkoptô**, 'I break up', used in military contexts in reference to bridges or roads. Paul has already mentioned (1.13) that he has been prevented so far from visiting Rome.

[23] 'Since there is no more scope', **mêketi topon echôn**, literally, 'no longer having a place'. As we have no evidence,

we cannot know precisely why Paul felt that there was no more scope for evangelization by him 'in this area', **en tois klimasi toutois**. This may refer to the place from which Paul is writing, either Ephesus or Corinth, or the general area of the Eastern Mediterranean. For the significance of the geographical term **klimata** see my notes on Gal. 1.21 in *Reading through Galatians*.

'Longing', **epipothiân,** is found nowhere else in the NT. It is the noun formed from the verb **epipotheô** which occurs in 1.11 in reference to the same topic.

[24] 'To be helped . . . on my way', **propemphthênai,** literally, 'to be escorted'.

'To some extent', **apo merous,** literally, 'in part', AV 'somewhat', NEB 'for a while'. Paul probably means that he would like to enjoy their company, even though it will only be a short visit and he will not have enough time to meet everybody.

'Have my fill of your company', **hûmôn . . . emplêsthô,** literally, 'be filled up with you', Vulg. *vobis . . . fruitus fuero,* i.e. 'enjoy you'.

[25] In the service of', literally, 'serving', **diâkonôn.**

[26] 'Macedonia and Achaea' were not the only areas which were making a contribution, since we know from I Cor. 16.1 that Galatia also was involved, and we can presume that the Christian churches in the rich province of Asia too would be generous. Paul probably mentions Macedonia and Achaea because they were the areas where he would begin collecting the money at the start of his journey to Jerusalem. This fits in with the tradition that Paul wrote this letter in Corinth which is in the province of Achaea.

'Have decided', **eudokêsan,** carries the sense of being pleased to do something, i.e. 'have consented', 'approved of'.

'Make a contribution', **koinôniân poiêsasthai**, literally, 'to make a share'. This is the sense the word also carries in Heb. 13.16, 'Do not forget to do charitable works and *to share with others* (**koinôniâs**).'

'The poor among the saints'; see my notes on Gal. 2.10 in *Reading through Galatians*.

[27] The whole church, not only the Gentiles, owed everything to the founding church in Jerusalem, but the Gentiles are mentioned here particularly as debtors because their position in the new Israel, as Paul has outlined earlier, is a privilege given to them by God. They have been fortunate in being grafted on to the olive tree and should remember that the root bears them, not they the root (11.18).

'Spiritual blessings', **tois pneumatikois**, literally, 'the spiritual things'.

'Physical needs', **tois sarkikois**, literally, 'the fleshly things'.

[28] 'When I have . . . completed the delivery of', **sphrâgisamenos**, literally, 'having sealed'. This is clearly a term from commercial practice, but the precise metaphor is not clear. It could refer to marking with a seal goods for consignment, a common usage, or to the confirming of a completed transaction by the application of of a seal, i.e. 'setting a seal on', 'marking the end to'. The latter seems to fit better with the opening remark, 'when I have finished'.

'These proceeds', **ton karpon touton**, literally, 'this fruit'.

[29] 'With the full blessing of Christ' seems to be an abbreviated way of saying 'Christ will give me his full blessing and at the same time you will receive the benefit of this blessing'. Barrett puts a slightly different construction on the phrase and translates the last part as, 'I shall come to bring and to find a full measure of the blessing of Christ'. Paul, of

course, did visit Rome later, but in circumstances very different from those anticipated here.

30 I beseech you, brothers and sisters, through our Lord Jesus Christ and through the love of the Spirit to strive along with me in prayers to God on my behalf, 31 that I may be delivered from the unbelievers in Judaea and that my service to Jerusalem may be well received by the saints, 32 so that, with God's will, I may come to you in joy and have a time to rest with you. 33 May the God of peace be with you all, amen.

[30] 'To strive along with', **synagônisasthai**, literally, 'to struggle or contend with', a word found nowhere else in the NT, is derived from the noun **agôn**, a word frequently used to denote an athletic contest or similar forms of competition. The use of a **syn-** compound is characteristic of Paul's style, as I note in *Reading through Colossians and Ephesians* in reference to Col. 2.12; Eph. 2.6 and 3.6. 'Strive . . . in prayers' is echoed in Col. 4.12, 'He is at all times striving on your behalf in his prayers.'

[31] The 'unbelievers' are non-Christian Jews. The account of Paul's mission to Jerusalem in Acts 21 gives the background to this verse. The suspicion of Paul was not confined to non-Christian Jews, as we can guess from Paul's prayer that the contribution should be 'well received' by the 'saints'. He clearly feared that they might reject it.

[32] 'Have a time to rest with you', literally, 'rest together with you', **synanapausômai hûmîn**, is another **syn-** compound verb and another word found nowhere else in the NT. The Vulg. *refrigerer vobiscum* gives us the AV 'with you be refreshed'.

[33] This prayer closes the main body of the letter, but we need not assume that what follows does not belong to the letter. Paul frequently interjects prayers and uses the word 'amen' in places other than the end of his letters.

Chapter 16

1 I commend our sister Phoebe to you, who is also a deaconess of the church in Cenchreae, 2 so that you may welcome her in the Lord in a manner worthy of the saints and give her your assistance in any situation where she needs it. For indeed she has been herself a protector of many as well as of myself. 3 Greet Prisca and Aquila, my fellow workers in Christ Jesus, 4 who have risked their necks for my life, to whom not only I, but all the churches of the Gentiles, are grateful, 5 and [greet] the church in their house. Greet my beloved Epainetus, the first fruit of Asia for Christ. 6 Greet Mary, who has toiled hard on your behalf. 7 Greet Andronicus and Junias, my kinfolk and fellow prisoners, who are outstanding among apostles and who were in Christ before I was. 8 Greet my beloved Ampliatus in the Lord. 9 Greet Urbanus our fellow worker in Christ and my beloved Stachys. 10 Greet Apelles, well-tried in Christ, greet those of the household of Aristoboulus.

Is this section, which consists mainly of a list of salutations, part of the original letter, or has it been detached from another one? It would be beyond the scope of this guide to detail all the arguments used by both sides in this controversy, but I will briefly go through some of the main points.

Those who argue that this section does not belong here do so on the following grounds:

1. Paul is unlikely to have known so many people in Rome, a place which he had never visited.
2. Some of the names are associated with Ephesus rather than Rome.
3. Some early manuscripts apparently did not include chapter 16.

These arguments are countered as follows:

1. It is pure supposition to say that Paul could not have known the names of so many people in Rome. It is likely that there were far more Christians in Rome than any other city in the Gentile world, with the possible exception of Antioch or Alexandria, especially as we know that they were established there at a very early period. Furthermore, Paul is clearly concerned to establish links with them and would have been careful to find out the names of as many people as possible. We do not have to accept that he must have met all of them, although the list does include the names of people whom he had definitely met elsewhere and who had subsequently gone to Rome. It is often forgotten how freely people travelled throughout the Roman empire and how easy it was for Paul to have learned a great deal about what was happening in the Christian communities throughout the area.

2. Although a few of the people in this list are known to have stayed in Ephesus at some time, there is no reason to assume that they were not living in Rome at the time the letter was written. Prisca and Aquila, for example, who had been expelled from Rome originally during the reign of the emperor Claudius, as we know from Acts 18.2, had met Paul in Corinth and travelled with him to Ephesus. It is more than likely that they subsequently returned to Rome along with

other Jews when Claudius' ban was repealed, probably some time after his death in 54. The existence of so many Greek, as against Latin, names is no evidence for claiming that they could not have been living in Rome. Greek names were very common in Rome, especially among slaves and freedmen. I shall attempt to show that some of these names definitely point to a Roman provenance. Finally, the hypothesis that this section belongs to a letter written to the church in Ephesus rests upon the assumption either that such a letter existed and that it had become detached from that letter and attached to this one, or that the letter to the Romans was actually addressed to more than one church and that this list of names comes from the version of the letter which was sent to Ephesus. Needless to say, these speculations are totally unsupported by any firm evidence.

3. All our manuscripts include this section. We know from early authorities such as Origen (*Commentary on Romans* in the Latin version by Rufinus, in reference to 16.25–27) that the heretic Marcion did not use chapter 16 (or chapter 15, for that matter), but Marcion was given to using specially doctored versions of Paul's letters.

In conclusion, most scholars today believe that the list of names is authentic and many believe that it belongs to this letter. At the same time, it is not crucial to the understanding of Romans if the list is omitted. It would certainly have become increasingly irrelevant to the reader as time passed and the original persons named were forgotten.

[1] 'I commend', **synistêmi**, a verb used when introducing or recommending one person to another.

'Sister', i.e. 'fellow Christian'.

'Deaconess', **diâkonon**, rather than simply 'servant', because the use of this word here probably denotes a particular function. We can presume that Phoebe was carrying this letter to Rome. Whether this was the only reason for her visit we do not know. As to her designation as 'deaconness', we know from Pliny (Book 10, letter 96), who, in order to extract information, tortured two 'servants, who were called "ministrae" (the Latin equivalent of **diâkonoi**)', *ancillis, quae ministrae dicebantur*, that by the start of the second century the office of 'deaconness' seems already to be established. Phoebe's name ('Shining') seems to be a pagan one, used by Roman poets in particular as a title of the goddess Diana.

'Cenchreae' is the south-east port of Corinth.

[2] 'Give . . . assistance', **parastête**, literally, 'stand by', Vulg. *assistatis*.

'Protector', **prostatis**, the feminine form of **prostatês**, literally, 'one who stands before', hence a guardian or champion. There is no need to assume that this is a title denoting some official or legal position.

[3] Prisca and Aquila, as I have mentioned above, met Paul in Corinth. They happened to share his profession, being **skênopoioi** (Acts 18.3), normally translated as 'tent makers', but more accurately described as 'makers of canopies and awnings'. The diminutive form of Prisca's name, 'Priscilla', is the one by which she is known in Acts. Barclay sees both as connected with the Roman family of Acilius Glabrio, whose name sometimes is written as Aquilius, a family in which the female name of Prisca was common. He speculates that Prisca may even have been a member by birth of that family and that this higher social standing is the reason why she is named before her Jewish husband.

[4] We do not know to which particular incident Paul is referring, but there were many times in Corinth and in Ephesus when Prisca and Aquila could have been involved in a dangerous situation along with Paul.

[5] Epainetus's description as **aparchê**, 'first fruit', a word we have met in 8.23 and 11.16, implies that he was the first of Paul's converts in the province of Asia (some manuscripts have 'Achaea' instead of 'Asia'), which is, of course, only a part of the area we know as Asia Minor. We know nothing about him apart from this reference, but he may have moved to Rome along with Prisca and Aquila. We certainly cannot prove from his presence in the list of names that this letter was written to the church in Ephesus.

[6] 'Mary', **Mariân**, occurs in several manuscripts as **Mariam**, which would indicate that she was Jewish, but it has been suggested that the name may be Latin, i.e. a feminine form of Marius.

'Toiled hard', **polla ekopiasen**, is a strong expression, i.e. 'has tired herself out greatly'.

'On your behalf', **eis hûmâs**, literally, 'in regard to you'. There is an alternative reading **hêmâs**, 'us', followed by the AV, but the majority of good manuscripts have **hûmâs**. There is also a reading **en hûmîn**, 'among you', Vulg. *in vobis*, but it also is not well supported.

[7] 'Junias', **Iouniân**, which could also be feminine 'Junia', appears in some manuscripts as **Iouliân**, 'Julia', probably because the latter was a much commoner name.

'My kinfolk', **tous syngeneis mou**, not the NEB 'my fellow-countrymen', because that would mean only they were from Cilicia, not that they were related to Paul, which is what the term must mean. Nor does it mean 'fellow-Jews', as Barrett suggests, because other Jews mentioned by Paul are not described as **syngeneis**. Either they were of Paul's tribe, Benjamin, or they were more closely related. Despite their Gentile names, they are certainly Jewish Christians.

'Fellow prisoners', **synaichmalôtous**, literally, 'fellow prisoners of war'. It need not be a metaphorical reference, i.e.

'conquered by Christ', since they may have been imprisoned at some time by the authorities along with Paul.

'Among apostles', i.e. 'as apostles', rather than 'in the estimation of the apostles'. The term 'apostle' can be used loosely to refer to anyone who has been 'sent out' to spread the gospel, without necessarily referring to the group we know as the 'Apostles'.

[8–10] We know nothing certain of Ampliatus, whose name in some manuscripts is 'Amplias', clearly an abbreviated form, but, according to Dodd (Introduction, 23), he could be the one whose tomb survives in the cemetery of Domitilla (see note on v. 15) on the Via Ardeatina. Nor do we know anything about Urbanus, Apelles or Stachys. The name of the last person mentioned, 'Ear of Corn' or 'Crop', points to his being a slave. It is also, incidentally, the name of the chief star in the constellation of Virgo. Apelles is probably a Hellenized form of 'Abel' and is found as a name for Jews elsewhere, most famously in its Latin form 'Apella', in Horace (*Satires*, I, 5,100, 101): *credat Iudaeus Apella, non ego*, 'let the Jew Apella believe it – I don't'.

'Of the household of Aristoboulus', **ek tôn Aristoboulou**, literally, 'of those of Aristoboulus'. He need not be a Christian; we only know that there were some Christians in his household, probably slaves. He could have been a grandson of Herod the Great who lived in Rome during the reign of Claudius, but again this is mere supposition.

11 Greet Herodion my kinsman. Greet those of the household of Narcissus who are in the Lord. 12 Greet Tryphaena and Tryphosa who toil in the Lord. Greet my beloved Persis who has toiled hard in the Lord. 13 Greet Rufus, chosen in the Lord, and his mother, who is also mine. 14 Greet Asyncritus, Phlegon, Hermes,

Patrobas, Hermas and the brethren with them. 15
Greet Philologus and Julia, Nereus and his sister, and
Olympas and all the saints with them. 16 Greet one
another with a holy kiss. All the churches of Christ
greet you.

[11] 'Herodion' may be connected with the household of
Aristoboulus, hence his name, which recalls Herod. For
'kinsman' see the note on v. 7.

Narcissus may be the famously wealthy freedman and
secretary of Claudius, who committed suicide and whose
property ended up in the hands of Nero, Claudius' successor.
His slaves and servants would have still been referred to as
'the household of Narcissus' after his death.

[12] Tryphaena and Tryphosa are names derived from the
Greek verb **tryphaô**, 'I am delicate', 'I live extravagantly', 'I
give myself airs'. There is a certain irony in the fact that Paul
describes them as 'toiling'. If not related, they must at least
have been slaves from the same household.

Persis, 'the Persian woman', need not have come from
Persia. For 'toiled hard' see the note on v. 6.

[13] Rufus may be the son of Simon of Cyrene, who was
compelled to carry Jesus' cross. In Mark 15.21 Simon is
described as 'the father of Alexander and Rufus', which
means that Rufus (and Alexander) must have been known
by those for whom that Gospel was written. Barclay
suggests that Mark's Gospel was written for the church in
Rome and so they would know who Rufus was. Paul must
have known Rufus very well for him to describe Rufus'
mother as 'also mine'. An Alexander, incidentally, turns up
in Ephesus (Acts 19.33) as a defender of Paul during the riot
in the theatre.

[14] These names, which are all Greek, seem to belong to one house church, just as those in the next verse seem to belong to another. Asyncritus, 'Incomparable', and Phlegon, 'Blazing', must be slaves. The name Hermas is given to the main character, described as the slave of a woman called Rhoda, of *The Shepherd*, a second-century Christian work which is set in Rome and its neighbourhood. Nothing, however, is known of any of the people mentioned here.

[15] 'Philologus', 'Lover of words', may have been a school teacher or tutor. Olympas is probably an abbreviation for Olympiodorus, just as Hermas in the previous verse is probably short for Hermodorus. See my note on Col. 4.15 regarding 'Nymphas' in *Reading through Colossians and Ephesians*. None of these persons are known, but Barclay suggests that Nereus could have been the same Nereus who was in the household of Flavius Clemens, a prominent Roman who was executed around 95 apparently for his Christianity, i.e. 'atheism'. His wife Flavia Domitilla, a niece of the emperor Domitian, was exiled on the same grounds. The early Christian cemetery referred to above is connected with her.

[16] The formula 'Greet one another with a holy kiss' is also found in I Cor. 16.20 and II Cor. 13.12. In I Thess. 5.26 Paul says, 'Greet *all the brethren* with a holy kiss', and in I Peter 5.14 we have 'Greet one another with *a kiss of love*'. It seems to be a common way of ending letters in the early church. As Justin Martyr describes (*Apology* I, 65.2), the kiss was incorporated into the liturgy.

17 I beseech you, brothers and sisters, to watch out for those creating dissensions and stumbling blocks contrary to the teaching which you received, and avoid them. 18 For such people are not servants of our

Lord Christ but of their own bellies, and through their fair words and fine language deceive the hearts of the innocent. 19 For your [reputation for] obedience has reached everyone, and I rejoice over you, but I want you to be wise in regard to what is good and pure in regard to evil. 20 The God of peace will speedily beat down Satan under your feet. May the grace of our Lord Jesus be with you.

[17] Some commentators are disturbed by the interruption of the list of salutations with this warning against wicked teachers, but it is not, in fact, really an interruption, since it comes after a list of people in Rome *to whom* Paul is sending greetings, and before a list of people with Paul *from whom* greetings are being sent. It may seem abrupt, but it is quite normal for Paul suddenly to introduce a new thought or to return to a previous topic without warning.

'Dissensions', **dichostasiâs**, occurs in one other place in the NT, Gal. 5.20, along with such other 'works of the flesh' as 'intrigues' and 'sectarianism'.

'You received', **emathete**, literally, 'you learned'.

[18] These people are described as 'servants of their own bellies', as Barrett points out, not because they are gluttons, but because they are preoccupied with food laws. In other words, they are treating the dietary commandments of the Law as more important than faith in Christ. Nor is it because they are preaching their doctrines in return for pay. Compare Phil. 3.18, 19, 'enemies of the cross of Christ, whose end is destruction, whose God is their belly'. These are clearly similar to the false teachers whom Paul denounces in II Cor. 11.4–15.

'Fair words', **chrêstologiâs**, and 'fine language', **eulogiâs**, are practically synonyms. **Chrêstologiâ** occurs nowhere else in the NT, but **eulogiâ** is common, usually in the sense of 'blessing', as in 15.29.

[19] 'Obedience', **hypakoê**; see notes on 1.5 and 6.16. Paul seems to be implying that their faithful obedience and enthusiastic acceptance of the gospel made them vulnerable to those who might lead them astray.

'Pure', **akeraious**, literally, 'unmixed', 'uncontaminated', hence 'guileless'.

[20] The manuscripts have many variant readings from this point on. For instance, the grace given here is found in some manuscripts also as v. 24, with the addition of 'Christ . . . all, amen', a repetition followed by the AV; in others it occurs after v. 27, perhaps because it was felt to be in the wrong place. The best manuscripts, however, have it only here.

21 Timothy, my fellow worker, greets you, together with Lucius, Jason and Sosipater, my kinfolk. 22 I, Tertius, who wrote this letter, greet you in the Lord. 23 Gaius, [who is] my host and [the host] of the whole church, greets you. Erastus the city treasurer and Quartus our brother [also greet you]. 24 (May the grace of our Lord Jesus Christ be with you all, amen.) 25 To him who can strengthen you according to my gospel and the preaching of Jesus Christ, according to the revelation of the secret which has been kept in silence for eternal ages, 26 but has been manifested now and, through the writings of the prophets, following the commandment of the eternal God, has been made known for the hearing of the faith to all the Gentiles, 27 to the only wise God, through Jesus Christ, to whom be glory for ever, amen.

[21] Now we meet someone who is very familiar. Timothy's name occurs throughout the letters and Acts. He is the son of a Jewish mother; Paul circumcised him in Galatia for his work with Jews, and he went with Paul to Macedonia and Achaea. He later accompanied Paul to Asia at the start of Paul's final journey to Jerusalem. Lucius has been identified with Luke, and it is possible that this identification is correct, but he could be the same Lucius of Cyrene who is mentioned in Acts 13.1 as one of those who laid hands on Paul and Barnabas at Antioch before their missionary trip to Cyprus. Jason is probably the same Jason who accepted Paul's teaching after hearing him preach in his synagogue in Thessalonica (Acts 17.7), and as a result was denounced to the authorities by other Jews. Sosipater could be the person named Sopater of Beroea in Acts 20.4.

For 'my kinfolk' see note on v. 7.

[22] Although Tertius is not mentioned elsewhere, he could be the same scribe who wrote Galatians. Käsemann thinks that the fact that he sends personal greetings proves that he must be known to the recipients. This does not follow.

[23] Gaius is possibly the same Gaius whom Paul baptized in Corinth (I Cor.1.14), or the Macedonian Gaius who was with Paul in Ephesus (Acts 19.29), or the Gaius of Derbe who accompanied Paul along with Timothy and Sopater on his last trip to Asia (Acts 20.4). It is a very common name. Erastus is probably the same one who was in Ephesus with Timothy when Paul sent them both to Macedonia (Acts 19.22), and who is mentioned as staying in Corinth in II Tim. 4.20. 'City treasurer' may sound an elevated title, but slaves and freed-men frequently held such secretarial posts. Quartus is un-known; his description as 'brother' means simply that he was a fellow Christian.

[24] See note on v. 20.

[25] We now come to the final doxology. As I state in the introduction, in some manuscripts it comes at the end of chapter 14, in others it occurs in both places, one has it after chapter 15, and two omit it altogether. This may merely indicate, as I point out there, that more than one version of the letter was in circulation. A more serious argument against the authenticity of this doxology is that it is couched in a language which is quite different from that which is generally regarded as Pauline. This argument, however, seems to depend largely on a rather select view of what constitutes Pauline writing. If we exclude Ephesians, Colossians and the Pastoral letters from the Pauline corpus, we will obviously find fewer echoes of Paul's style and vocabulary in this section. There is a word which occurs nowhere else in Paul and two phrases found nowhere else in the NT, but arguing from **hapax legomena** (see *Reading through Colossians and Ephesians*, 3, 4) can be dangerous. It may be that Paul incorporated into his doxology phrases which had been composed by someone else and which were familiar to his audience, but, although I have reservations about it, I would hesitate to dismiss the whole doxology as a later composition which was attached to this letter perhaps to provide a more imposing conclusion. There is not enough evidence to support a dogmatic position on this question.

'Strengthen', **stêrixai**, recalls 1.11, 'some spiritual blessing which will strengthen you'.

'The preaching of Jesus Christ', **to kêrygma Iêsou Christou**, explains 'my gospel', i.e. it is Paul's preaching about Christ.

'Secret', **mystêriou**, is God's hidden purpose which is now revealed, i.e. the inclusion of the Gentiles in his plan of salvation. There is no difference between the use of this word here and its use elsewhere in Paul. It occurs not only in 11.25 but also six times in the contemporary letter I Corinthians, so it can hardly be described as a word only associated with such later works as Colossians and Ephesians.

'Kept in silence', **sesîgêmenou,** the only instance of this verb being used in the passive in the NT, although this usage is not uncommon in Greek literature.

'Eternal ages', **chronois aiôniois,** is a phrase found also in II Tim. 1.9 and Titus 1.2.

[26] 'Writings of the prophets', **graphôn prophêtikôn,** literally 'the prophetic writings', is unique in this form, i.e. using the adjective, in the NT, but Matt. 26.56, 'All this happened so that *the writings of the prophets* (**hai graphai tôn prophêtôn**) might be fulfilled', has a very similar phrase.

'Eternal God', **aiôniou Theou,** is another phrase found nowhere else in the NT, but other phrases incorporating the adjective **aiônios** are also found occurring as unique examples, e.g. 'everlasting encouragement' in II Thess. 2.16 and 'eternal covenant' in Heb. 13.20.

'For the hearing of the faith', **eis hypakoên pisteôs,** is found also in 1.5, where we also have the phrase 'among all the nations', which corresponds to 'to all the Gentiles (i.e. nations)' here. See the notes on that verse. This recalls the opening assertion of the letter that God has revealed salvation through his Son to all the world and that Paul himself has been appointed by God to preach this gospel.

[27] 'Only wise God', **monôi sophôi Theôi,** is a phrase easily misunderstood. It does not mean that God is the only wise God, and that all the other gods are stupid, but rather that God is the only being who is wise. But it also implies that there is only one God, and that he is wise. In I Tim. 1.17, 'To the king of the ages, the immortal, invisible, only God, be honour and glory, for ever and ever', appears in some manuscripts with the addition of 'wise' after 'only', but it is likely that this variation was due to a confusion with the phrase in Romans,

Bibliography

The following list represents a tiny fraction of the material available on the subject. I found some of the books listed very useful, others less so. No conclusion should be drawn from the fact that some famous works do not appear in this bibliography. I have simply noted those to which I make reference while writing this book.

W. Barclay, *The Letter to the Romans*, The Saint Andrew Press, Edinburgh 1955

C. K. Barrett, *A Commentary on the Epistle to the Romans*, A. & C. Black, London 1957

J. C. Beker, *Paul the Apostle*, T. & T. Clark, Edinburgh 1980

C. H. Dodd, *The Epistle of Paul to the Romans*, The Moffatt New Testament Commentary, Hodder and Stoughton, London 1932

K. P. Donfried (ed.), *The Romans Debate*, T. & T. Clark, Edinburgh 1991

E. Käsemann, *Commentary on Romans*, translated from the German by G. W. Bromiley, SCM Press, London 1980

J. B. Lightfoot, *Notes on Epistles of St Paul*, Macmillan, London 1895

J. A. T. Robinson, *Wrestling with Romans*, SCM Press, London 1979

W. Sanday & A. C. Headlam, *A Critical and Exegetical Commentary on the Epistle to the Romans*, T. & T. Clark, Edinburgh ⁵1902

K. Stendahl, *Paul among Jews and Gentiles*, SCM Press, London 1977

A. J. M. Wedderburn, *The Reasons for Romans*, T. & T. Clark, Edinburgh 1988

T. Wright, *What Saint Paul Really Said*, Lion Publishing, Oxford 1997 and so it seems to be the case that God is described as **monos** elsewhere in the NT, but never as **sophos**. This is not significant, however, since references to the 'wisdom', **sophia**, of God are common.

'To whom' is strictly speaking redundant, since we already have a dative 'to God'. Some manuscripts replace 'to whom' with 'to him', but it is likely that the original text did have 'to whom'; perhaps the author meant to say 'to the only wise God, through Jesus Christ, be glory, and to Jesus Christ also be glory'.